Robe of Light

Robe of Light

An Esoteric Christian Cosmology

Swami Nirmalananda Giri
(Abbot George Burke)

Light of the Spirit
Press
Cedar Crest. New Mexico

Published by

    Light of the Spirit Press
    lightofthespiritpress.com

    Light of the Spirit Monastery
    P. O. Box 1370
    Cedar Crest, New Mexico 87008
    ocoy.org

ISBN-13: 978-0-9985998-0-9
ISBN-10: 0-9985998-0-8

Library of Congress Control Number: 2017900569
Light of the Spirit Press, Cedar Crest, NEW MEXICO

1. REL062000 RELIGION / Spirituality
2. REL047000 RELIGION / Mysticism
3. REL068000 RELIGION / Theosophy

First edition, (February 2017)

05162024

CONTENTS

ILLUSTRATIONS

Robe of Light

An Esoteric Christian Cosmology

O Lord my God, thou coverest thyself with light as with a garment (Psalms 104:2).

Thou, Lord, in the beginning hast laid the foundation of the earth; and the heavens are the works of thine hands: They shall perish; but thou remainest; and they all shall wax old as doth a garment; And as a vesture shalt thou fold them up, and they shall be changed: but thou art the same (Hebrews. 1:10-12).

The basic pattern

"Where am I?… How did I get here?" is more than a trite line from nineteenth century melodramas and novels. It is a query put forth by potential sages throughout the history of conscious mankind. When asked on a cosmic scale, it is bold indeed: *What is this universe I keep finding*

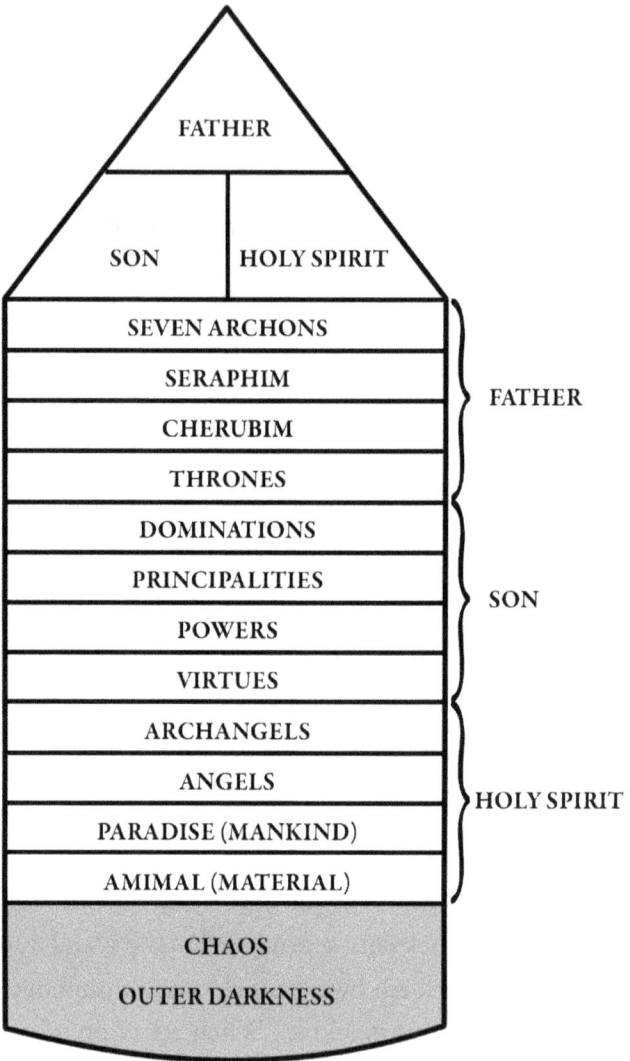

myself in, and how did I get here? That is answered by an esoteric Christian cosmology.

The preceding illustration indicates how things develop in the divine pattern. At the top is a triangle bearing the divine symbolic titles of Father, Son, and Holy Spirit–the Triune Unity, the Trinity.

Immediately below the triangle is a section labeled "Seven Archons." These are the seven great creators who project and direct the universe. We read about them in the book of Revelation: "Grace be unto you, and peace, from him which is, and which was, and which is to come; and from the seven Spirits which are before his throne" (Revelation 1:4). "These things saith he that hath the seven Spirits of God" (Revelation 3:1). "And there were seven lamps of fire burning before the throne, which are the seven Spirits of God" (Revelation 4:5). "In the midst of the elders, stood a Lamb as it had been slain, having seven horns and seven eyes, which are the seven Spirits of God sent forth into all the earth" (Revelation 5:6).

These are the seven greatest and most highly evolved beings in existence, so near to Divinity that they might even be called the seven fingers of God since their consciousnesses are to so great a degree merged with God. Only the slightest tinge of separate consciousness remains in them so they may carry out the divine creative plan. Yet so nearly total is their oneness with God's Consciousness that their wills are flawless reflections of the divine will and their actions are truly acts of God. With God as their inmost guide, they project the entire universe from the most subtle to the grossest realms and enclose all conscious entities in those body vehicles which correspond to their individual levels of evolutional development. The principal thing to realize in all this is that in the final summation of things there is really only one source of the entire creation: God.

Naturally, the question arises: Why is God the source of all this? Why has God projected all these worlds and their inhabitants? The following is an explanation by esoteric Christianity.

The eternal impulse

All conscious beings have existed eternally within the being of God, the "bosom of the Father" (John 1:18), living within the heart of God, one with him, distinct though not separate. Having their essential being rooted in the infinity of God, the individual consciousnesses have within them a natural impulse to transcend their finitude and attain the boundlessness of their origin. This, of course, is impossible, since the essential, eternal nature of a being cannot be altered. Being rooted in God, and therefore in a sense a part of God, all beings are as immutable as God, the only infinite Being. Yet the urge for transcendence is part of their essential nature.

The solution

The solution to this dilemma is actually quite simple: the individual consciousnesses cannot alter their natural state of finitude, but they can come to share and participate in the infinite consciousness of God. That is, they cannot become infinite themselves, but they can experience the infinity of another–their divine Father-Source. This is symbolized in the Scriptures by the expressions regarding their coming to sit in the throne of the Father or becoming heirs of His kingdom. "Jesus said unto them, Verily I say unto you,… ye also shall sit upon twelve thrones" (Matthew 19:28). "To him that overcometh will I grant to sit with me in my throne, even as I also overcame, and am set down with my Father in his throne" (Revelation 3:21). "Hath not God chosen the poor of this world rich in faith, and heirs of the kingdom which he hath promised to them that love him?" (James 2:5). "Come, ye blessed of my Father, inherit the kingdom prepared for you from the foundation of the world" (Matthew 25:34). "The Spirit itself beareth witness with our spirit, that we are the children of God: And if children, then heirs; heirs of God, and joint-heirs with Christ" (Romans 8:16,17). "That the Gentiles should be fellowheirs, and of the same body, and partakers of his promise in Christ by the gospel" (Ephesians 3:6).

Just as a psychically sensitive person can experience the thoughts and feelings of another by tuning in to him, yet in no way becoming that other person, so the individual consciousness can come to experience the Consciousness of God while remaining in its limited native state. It is necessary, however, for the individual spirit to develop the capacity for such a state of awareness. And this is done by learning to fully experience the state of existence of a being completely different from oneself–to enter into an alien mode of being altogether, while retaining the awareness of one's true identity. In other words, the individual spirit must learn to put on the "costume" of a consciousness utterly different from its own and become able not just to fully experience that other mode of consciousness, but also to develop the ability to function as that other kind of being.

Evolutionary creation

To enable the spirits to enter into this process, God breathes forth–emanates–his own self as the Son and the Holy Spirit and manifests all the realms of relative existence, from the most subtle worlds of the Cherubim and Seraphim to the most objective worlds of atomic matter. The spirits then enter into relative existence by taking on bodies of varying grades and patterns of vibratory energies and finally descending into this material world to begin working their way back up the ladder of ever-evolving forms, beginning with forms whose scope of consciousness is much lesser than theirs and working their way upward, entering into higher and higher levels of awareness until they can surpass their original breadth of consciousness and begin to partake of a life of awareness much beyond their own. Upward and upward they evolve until their capacity for awareness is developed to such a perfect state that they can actually experience the state of being of the Son and the Holy Spirit. Then, after having perfected themselves in even that empyrean state, they can actually reenter the Bosom of the Father in full participation of his all-embracing consciousness, thenceforth to live in his infinity, his ultimate gift of love to them, thus experiencing the meaning of his ancient declaration: "I am… thy exceeding great reward" (Genesis 15:1).

As Shakespeare wrote, "all the world's a stage" with the individual spirits wearing their costumes and playing their parts. Just as actors begin with small parts and progress to bigger roles by demonstrating their skill in those smaller parts, so also do the spirits advance to higher and more complex forms of existence and consciousness through taking on and perfecting their identity and functions within the evolutionary forms of creation, at last returning home to God.

Because of the incalculable length of time this process of return requires, God breathes forth the creation many times in cycles, as is indicated by the biblical statement: "Of old hast thou laid the foundation of the earth: and the heavens are the work of thy hands. They shall perish, but thou shalt endure: yea, all of them shall wax old like a garment; as a vesture shalt thou change them, and they shall be changed" (Psalms 102:25-26). The Apostle in his quotation of this passage uses the simile, "As a vesture shalt thou fold them up, and they shall be changed" (Hebrews 1:12). Creation, being an activity of the eternal God, is also eternal. It never began, and will never end. Instead, it runs in alternating cycles of manifestation-projection and withdrawal. Nothing is destroyed, simply recycled.

Looking back at the diagram, the utmost limit of His breathing out is the material plane. The first "character" in the cosmic drama as it unfolds is a single atom of hydrogen. This is the first body, the first "role" in which the newly-projected spirit finds itself. Then in its implanted will, tending back to the divine, it builds more and more complex atomic and molecular structures in the struggle to manifest full self-awareness. This entails an almost infinitely long series of progressively more complex and evolved body vehicles–each of which the spirit must both project around itself and function in to attain and manifest the fullest consciousness possible in those vehicles. As Oliver Wendel Holmes wrote in his poem, The Chambered Nautilus:

> Build thee more stately mansions, O my soul!
> As the swift seasons roll!
> Leave thy low-vaulted past!
> Let each new temple, nobler than the last,
> Shut thee from heaven with a dome more vast,
> Till thou at length art free,
> Leaving thine outgrown shell by life's unresting sea!

The drama of creation, simply stated, is this: God breathes forth this vast universe. Slowly it comes out and evolves according to set patterns. Then after a precise measure of time, he breathes it back in again, involves it, and it vanishes. This he does eternally. Mostly the same actors are in the successive dramas, though they evolve to bigger and (hopefully) better roles. This is expressed in the following words: "For the earnest expectation of the creature (*ktisis*–creation) waiteth for the manifestation of the sons of God.... For we know that the whole creation groaneth and travaileth in pain together until now" (Romans 8:19, 22). The creation is a living entity which labors–has birth pains–for the delivering of the sons of God, the individual spirits, from their involvement with and subsequent bondage in matter. Of those who finally climb the ladder of evolution to its pinnacle, the Lord Jesus says in Revelation: "Him that overcometh will I make a pillar in the temple of my God, and he shall go no more out" (Revelation 3:12). This is the state indicated by the term "salvation" (*soteria*).

God breathes forth himself as creation, and the individual spirit comes down and, as just said, is first of all embodied in an atom of hydrogen. As time passes, it builds more and more complex atomic and molecular structures. From gas to mineral to plant to animal–so develops the career of the individual spirit's drama of evolution. As the Sufi poet, Rumi, wrote:

A stone I died and rose again a plant.
A plant I died and rose an animal;
I died an animal and was born a man.
Why should I fear? What have I lost by death?
As man, death sweeps me from this world of men
That I may wear an angel's wings in heaven;
Yet e'en as angel may I not abide,
For nought abideth save the face of God.
Thus o'er the angels' world I wing my way
Onwards and upwards, unto boundless lights;
Then let me be as nought, for in my heart
Rings as a harp-song that we must return to Him.

At all stages along the way, we find organisms in which the differing levels overlap. In the sea we find entities which are simultaneously plant and animal, and on land we have those that have developed an elementary sense of touch and locomotion, such as the Venus flytrap. In human form there are those who are to some degree still animal. In the intervals between embodiments, the spirit spends time in the astral and causal regions where awakening and growth also take place. (This is best explained in the forty-third chapter of *Autobiography of a Yogi* by Paramhansa Yogananda.)

The normal state of things

The physical world in a normal universe is not as grossly material as our world is. Moreover, there is no disease, suffering, or death–no distortion of the divine pattern. The Fathers of the early Church believed that the parable of the Good Shepherd indicated that our world alone had gone awry, requiring the Incarnation for its restoration to the "fold" of normal evolution.

In the normal scheme of things (and our world at present is not normal), when the individual comes to the point where he has manifested to the fullest extent the levels of consciousness possible for pre-human animal life on earth, he no longer incarnates on the physical plane, but graduates to the next level of creation which is known in the Bible as Paradise–the realm from which Adam and Eve fell, the intended world for evolving human life. This is a psychic-astral world that is subtler than the material world in its vibratory fabric, though it is very much like the earth. Just as ripe fruit falls naturally from a tree, so the spirit progresses to this next realm of evolution. Paradise is the true world of "men," so I have labeled it as such. There the five senses function in a heightened degree, and the "sixth sense" of intuition starts to manifest.

Paradise is the stage on which the self-conscious entity known as "man" first appears in the evolution-drama and from which he passes eventually to the next plane of angelic evolution. That Paradise is not a material place is shown by Jesus' promise to the thief: "Verily I say unto thee, To day shalt thou be with me in paradise" (Luke 23:43).

After Paradise, the spirits progress into the angelic world and from there to the archangelic world. They continue onward until they reach the highest region and from there become totally reunited with the Infinite.

This is the way of spirit-progression in a normal universe–and there are many universes existing simultaneously. But what happened to this one we find ourselves in? Lucifer.

The Three and the Seven

Momentarily, let us look back at the diagram. Not having done so before, here let me also explain that in this diagram I am only showing the major divisions. Within each of these realms of evolution there exist myriads of levels and types. This is why the Lord Jesus said: "In my Father's house are many mansions"(John 14:2).

On the right, three great divisions are marked, each embracing four of the levels of creation. These three divisions have a subtle, reflective connection with the Trinity: Father, Son, and Holy Spirit. These three greater divisions are in a sense creations unto themselves, with the principle "as above, so below" dictating their hierarchical structure–that is, each is ruled and enlivened by a Triumvirate of Powers, corresponding to the Trinity, which supervises the manifestation of that particular segment of creation. Directly under their command are Seven Powers, corresponding to the Seven Archons, who perform the actual dynamics of manifestation-projection. So in each of the three realms we have a trinity and a septenary as the ruling intelligences. And each of these is a reflection of its counterpart in the realms above. We may think of each of them as a transformer which steps down the cosmic power and consciousness as it flows into a lower level of creation from the one immediately above it. Thus the entire creation is a series of lesser and lesser reflections of the ultimate Powers.

Our flawed world

In a previous creation cycle one of these seven lesser archons though (comparatively) highly evolved was yet somehow flawed. And through this flaw he became negative, twisted, and spiritually insane–for conscious, deliberate evil is just that: spiritual insanity. In his madness he determined to wrest the power from the other six lesser archons and with their combined power then unseat the lesser triumvirate and himself become the creator and ruler of the lower creation. This is indicated in the Bible, where it is said: "How art thou fallen from heaven, O Lucifer, son of the morning!… For thou hast said in thine heart, I will ascend into heaven, I will exalt my throne above the stars of God:… I will ascend above the heights of the clouds; I will be like the most High" (Isaiah 14:12-14). We call him Lucifer, Bearer of Light, but that is a metaphoric name only.

Unfortunately, he was not alone in his folly. Under his influence, some archangels and many angels partook of his madness and rebellion, and with him they fell. However, their evolutionary status remained, giving them access to the archangelic and lesser levels. They could not ascend, but they could descend, so in their frustrated malice they turned their attention to the lower regions which they were still determined to in some way dominate and wrest from the control of the lesser triumvirate and septenary. Having been expelled from their positions in the upward stream of evolution, the righthand path, they committed themselves to the cause of de-evolution, the lefthand path, and the hindering of those spirits who were yet climbing up the evolutionary ladder beneath them.

Thus it was that in fury the evil intelligences under the marshal of Lucifer turned their eyes from the heights to which they had aspired in vain and cast their glances of malicious pride into the worlds below and descended to those worlds with the intent of stopping and, if possible, reversing the upward flight of their younger brothers to the higher regions. To this end they bent their natural creative powers, distorting the basic patterns of creation and thereby distorting as well the forms the spirits were meant to inhabit. In this way they threw out of balance the fundamental magnetism of the lower worlds, causing them to become eddies, whirling traps that caught the spirits in a deadly orbit of aberration, rather than the steps to higher consciousness they were intended to be.

Adam and Eve

But this did not all happen in a moment; it was the work of ages. The first step was the psychic ruin of Adam and Eve. The Luciferic rebellion occurred right at the beginning of a creation cycle. In the previous cycle the spirits that were in Paradise had graduated up to the next evolutionary step: the angelic world. Paradise was thus ready for its next inhabitants coming up from the animal evolution of the material universe.

The spirit at its initial outbreathing is polarized to–made in the image of–either the Divine Male or the Divine Female and pursues most, though not all, of its evolution through bodies of a corresponding polarity. All worlds are entered through some sort of birth process effected by male and female parents in that realm. Consequently the guiding intelligences, the Elohim, the creator-mothers, selected the most evolved male and female intelligences to be the channels for the birth into Paradise of the spirits evolving up from the material plane. These they introduced into paradisiacal bodies made in their images: male and female (see Genesis 1:26-27). After a period of growth and adjustment in that realm, these two would become the foreparents of the new human beings coming up from the earth plane.

At this critical time Lucifer entered Paradise, fully cognizant of the evolutionary situation. He had two aims: to prevent Adam and Eve from channeling the upward-evolving spirits into Paradise and to repolarize them into channels for descending, "fallen" spirits. That is, wishing to populate the worlds with his denizens, he needed to find channels for the evil angels to incarnate into those worlds, abandoning their angelic forms. Incarnate demons both in Paradise and on the earth were his desire. From there he would increase his dark populace through the distortion and entrapment of the other spirits in those worlds.

To effect this, he utilized the fundamental drive of the incarnate spirit: the striving for increasing degrees of consciousness, the divinely-implanted discontent which yearns for transcendence of whatever relative condition in which the consciousness finds itself confined. This innate urge had spurred Lucifer to his audacious striving to overreach the intervening steps of evolution and leap to a higher realm. It was in keeping with his colossal egotism that he would attempt to remake Adam and Eve into his own image by enticing them to commit the same folly, holding out to them the seductive promise: "Ye shall be as gods" (Genesis 3:5).

For the first time a human being heard that knowledge is power–nay, more: divinity. The faculties of reflection and conscience were not yet developed in Adam and Eve, for in their prior evolution on the earth plane such psychic mechanisms were unneeded, and they had not yet had time to grow into their new status in Paradise. So, having come from a world where life ostensibly depended on food, and where the senses were reliable guides to nourishment and pleasure, "the woman saw that the tree was good for food, and that it was pleasant to the eyes, and a tree to be desired to make one wise, she took of the fruit thereof, and did eat, and gave also unto her husband with her; and he did eat" (Genesis 3:6). In the eating, their consciousness was altered–this was for many reasons, some psychological and some purely (astral) physical–

and the altering unbalanced them, polarizing them to the backward and downward, earthward magnetism.

"And the eyes of them both were opened, and they knew that they were naked" (Genesis 3:7). Heretofore, in Paradise they had been clothed with an astral body of subtle spiritual light to enable them to forget their animal past and identify with their newly awakened minds and intelligence, rather than an external vehicle. As a result of their eating the fruit prematurely and effecting changes they were unready for–and consequently unable to cope with–instead of their awareness being expanded, it became contracted, impacted and coarsened so they could no longer be clothed in light, but became "naked" in their reversion to fully external consciousness. In this way they experienced the loss of heightened consciousness, which was the "death" they had been warned about but had misunderstood. The third chapter of Genesis shows us further aberrations they developed, including blaming one another and even God for their own actions. The ability to lie, to project a false "reality" and take refuge in it–to this had their creative powers already become bent.

Banished from Paradise

They were now unfit for the divine plan, but ready indeed for Lucifer's aspirations. To circumvent this, they

were banished from Paradise, thus breaking the link through which the earthly spirits could rise to Paradise and through which the evil angelic intelligences could descend to invade Paradise.

Now what was to become of them? They had evolved beyond animal forms and could not revert to them, yet they had turned back from Paradise to a degree of earthly consciousness. They had engineered themselves, with Lucifer's help, into an evolutionary cul-de-sac. This was not as good as Lucifer had hoped for, but it did ensure that no spirit presently on the earth plane would be able to get beyond it. Further, it put those spirits who were too advanced for animal evolution into a limbo of stagnation, unable to either turn back or go forward. In this way he had momentarily thwarted the divine will and brought a portion of the creation to a dead halt.

He could not safely stop there, however, so he and his invisible cohorts embarked on the course of subliminal distortion already mentioned. Through this distortion pain, disease, deformity, violence and death entered the earth plane and strove to become the norm. Spirits could no longer spend the needed time span in the organism whose level of awareness they were evolving in at the time. Instead, through repeated physical deaths, they were violently and painfully thrown out of a succession of the same type of bodies–a process that not only interrupted their evolution, but created in them the habit of desperate clinging to physical embodiment as an end in itself, rather than a means of passage to a higher mode of life. Fear of death became a primary drive, and since death originally was the gateway to those higher modes of life, this fear developed into fear of evolution itself, as well.

There is no need to further catalog the terrible results– we need only look about us and at ourselves to see them.

One thing that should be mentioned, though, is the introduction of the hideous condition of organisms killing one another and eating one another's bodies to sustain their own physical life. That this was not the original way is seen from the very first chapter of the Bible: "And God said, Behold, I have given you every herb bearing seed, which is upon the face of all the earth, and every tree, in the which is the fruit of a tree yielding seed; to you it shall be for meat. And to every beast of the earth, and to every fowl of the air, and to every thing that creepeth upon the earth, wherein there is life, I have given every green herb for meat: and it was so" (Genesis 1:29-30). More than any other, this aberration of eating the flesh of other beings polarizes an entity to the left-hand path, as it is a perfect imaging of the demonic psyche and will. The eating of another's flesh is a primary lesson in the Luciferian re-education of the entrapped intelligence, ensuring that if it does evolve it will be under the influence of Darkness, committed to the principle of life from the death of another–the ultimate parasitism of a demon.

The way it should be

Turning back from this ugly spectacle, let us again consider normal creation and evolution. In a normal creation the spirit descends into matter and there begins

22

to experience ever-more-complex forms of existence, evolving upward through an almost infinite number of levels until perfect union with the Divine Consciousness is gained. There is no pain, anxiety, or strain in any of this. Rather, it is a leisurely, joyous, conscious process, death being no more than a simple stepping out of a no-longer-needed vehicle when its full potential has been realized. It is a happy, assured journey upward back to the Bosom of God with never a moment's experience of estrangement, isolation, or separation from the Divine Life. Suffering is thus impossible to the journeying spirit.

The way it has become

Such is not the case in our present creation, where distortion is the norm. So extensive and deep-seated is the twisting of the universe that some religions have even held that it was created by an evil god whose delight is the suffering and bondage of spirits. This is erroneous, but we can certainly understand how such a view could be adopted (another example of how astray the unenlightened intellect can lead us). The divine pattern is still present, but the overlay of demonic illusion (including a lot of religion) is immeasurable, stifling the life of spirits. The earth plane has become a terrible trap filled with crippled, agonizing intelligences. And daily it increases. The reign of Lucifer is superficial, but to our shallow awareness it seems all-embracing. And therefore, since we believe it to be so, it is so for us until we break from that illusion.

One of the demonic lies accepted by our human race is the principle that suffering is necessary–that it "purifies" and "ennobles," even supposedly enabling us to know what happiness is. Christianity in both the East and West has succumbed to this evil voice, idolatrizing suffering as God's will, and repeating the absurd proposition that we can rise through suffering. Submission to suffering has come to be extolled as a supreme virtue, thereby turning what should goad us to transcendence into a perverse form of bondage.

One of the most dramatic portrayals of our condition is the Fifteenth Major Arcanum of the Tarot deck. There we see two people, male and female, in imagined bondage to the Devil. The chains that supposedly bind them are only looped loosely around their necks. All the pair need do is slip off the chains and walk away, for they are already free. But instead they accept their non-existent enslavement as real and even normal. We must realize that the power of bondage is within ourselves and, when turned about, becomes the power which effects our freedom. We bind and release ourselves–none other is able to do so.

THE DEVIL .

Reaction

What were God, the lesser triumvirate, and the lesser archons doing while all the foregoing was taking place? They had already prevented the permatizing of Adam and Eve in their aberrated state, in which they were potential channels for descending negative intelligences, by banishing them from the Paradise level. "And the Lord God said, Behold, the man is become as one of us, to know good and evil: and now, lest he put forth his hand,

and take also of the tree of life, and eat, and live for ever: Therefore the Lord God sent him forth from the garden of Eden, to till the ground from whence he was taken. So he drove out the man; and he placed at the east of the garden of Eden Cherubims, and a flaming sword which turned every way, to keep the way of the tree of life" (Genesis 3:22-24). But God is Love (I John 4:8), and the effect of love is healing. So God and His creative ministers set about to heal.

Adam and Eve were without embodiment, being fit neither for the material world nor the region of Paradise. They had evolved beyond the animal bodies of the earth but had "died" unto the higher bodies of Paradise. Under the direction of Divine Intelligence, the Elohim specially created physical bodies for the fallen pair. Since the human body was created specifically as a stop-gap, deluded humanity wars with the earth and lives as a thing apart rather than living in the natural ecological flow of things. Physically we are strangers to this earth and react to it with great unwisdom.

The special creation of the human body is indicated in a veiled manner by the scriptural account, "Unto Adam also and to his wife did the Lord God make coats of skins, and clothed them" (Genesis 3:21). The subsequent, sad story of Adam and Eve and their descendants can be read in the Bible. As the saga unfolds we see the patterns of Lucifer being woven more and more into the fabric of human life and history.

Were Paradise and the Garden of Eden the same thing? There seems to be an earthly locale indicated for the Garden in Genesis, although there is definitely a symbolic interpretation for this. Further, the account of the fall of man in Genesis is undoubtedly confused–perhaps scrambled. One theory put forth is that the tragedy of Paradise was once again repeated on earth in the Garden of Eden, which was modeled after the prototype of Paradise; that Lucifer descended to the earth and once again seduced our foreparents, plunging them into further chaos and estrangement from their evolutionary destiny. But this does not seem likely.

However we may choose to look at it, there is no denying that we are here–and in need.

The divine plan

"The world is mine, and the fulness thereof" (Psalms 50:12) is an unchangeable dictum. All things remain ever in the hand of God, whatever the appearances may be. This is why Saint Paul could say with confidence: "We know that all things work together for good to them that love God, to them who are the called according to his purpose" (Romans 8:28). Lucifer may have had long-range plans, but so did God.

He revealed this plan at the very beginning when saying to Lucifer: "I will put enmity between thee and the woman, and between thy seed and her seed; it shall bruise thy head, and thou shalt bruise his heel" (Genesis 3:15). The Latin Vulgate, one of the most ancient texts, and one that reflects the mind of the early church, gives this reading: "I will put enmities between thee and the woman, and thy seed and her seed; she shall crush thy head, and thou shalt lie in wait for her heel."

What does it mean? That God cannot be thwarted. The prime law of the universe is the law of evolution, the law of the inevitable flight of the spirit back to divinity. Lucifer may have grievously delayed that homeward flight, but never could he permanently stop it. For God has another basic law in His universe: "Whatsoever a man soweth, that shall he also reap. For he that soweth to his flesh shall of the flesh reap corruption; but he that soweth to the Spirit shall of the Spirit reap life everlasting" (Galatians 6:7-8).

What we do in the flesh we shall reap in the flesh—either in this present body or in a future body created for us by the forces we have set in motion by our previous deeds and desires. Today we reap the fruits of yesterday and sow the seeds of tomorrow. Those who do not know

this curse "blind fate" and even God for the supposedly
unjust suffering of the seemingly innocent. But if they
understood these two laws and realized that all which
happens to us is our own doing coming back to us, and
is for our eventual growth, their hearts' agonies would be
laid to rest. The bewildered mind may see only confused
darkness when viewing life and the world around it, but
"the light shines in the darkness" ultimately, revealing to
us the conjoined wisdom of God and our evolving spirit.
Suffering is the product of ignorance. Gnosis–knowledge
and understanding–brings peace.

"Fathers" and "children"

Inspired scriptures are often heavily symbolic. Two
such symbols are "fathers" and "children." "The Lord...
[is] by no means clearing the guilty, visiting the iniquity
of the fathers upon the children unto the third and fourth
generation" (Numbers 14:18). This seems to support
the contention that God permits–even causes–unjust
suffering in the world, but the light of understanding
dispels this misapprehension. "Father" is the term
applied to a body which engenders other, future bodies.
Thus, "father" symbolizes the body in, and by which, we
set in motion the forces of sowing and reaping through
our actions and our own creative will. In the Eastern

philosophies the term "karma" is used to designate these forces. "Children" symbolizes the future bodies "fathered" by the present body's actions. Through these "children" the embodied spirit reaps the results of the actions of its own previous "father" body.

In this verse from Numbers we find the phrase: "He by no means clears the guilty...." This is echoed by Saint Paul in his Galatians exposition: "Be not deceived; God is not mocked: for whatsoever a man soweth, that shall he also reap" (Galatians 6:7). In other words, the law of sowing and reaping is inexorable; no one can bend or get around it. The law of rebirth holds sway over all, for it is the obverse, the corollary, of the law of evolution.

Sentence of rebirths

We may seem to have strayed far from the third chapter of Genesis, but we have not. Rather, we are laying the foundation for a true understanding of those words to Lucifer: "I will put enmity between thee and the woman, and between thy seed and her seed; it shall bruise thy head, and thou shalt bruise his heel," and then to Eve: "I will greatly multiply thy sorrow and thy conception; in sorrow thou shalt bring forth children; and thy desire shall be to thy husband, and he shall rule over thee" (Genesis 3:16).

Let us analyze this latter verse according to the principles just outlined. In these words, God places Eve and Adam under the law of rebirth–to fulfill which "did the Lord God make coats of skins, and clothed them" in physical, earthly bodies that were suited to their state of evolution and appropriate vehicles for their sowing and reaping. "I will greatly multiply thy sorrow and thy conception" is a prophecy of the many sorrowful lives–births or conceptions–Eve and Adam would have to undergo in their journeying back to Paradise, reaping the consequences of their disobedient folly. For it was not themselves alone which they had plunged into an abyss of suffering and wandering from life to life, but all the spirits beneath them on the evolutionary ladder.

Not only had they halted the evolution of those spirits, they had ensured nothing but suffering embodiments for them and the even more terrible evil of ingrained susceptibility to demonic influence and distortion. The abyss of hell yawned not only at the feet of the primal pair, but for all spirits striving upward in what would now be an almost futile prolonged struggle. The negative effect of their disobedience was literally cosmic. No wonder, then, that God further said to Eve: "In sorrow thou shalt bring forth children."

The promise of hope

But He did not leave her with only this prospect of future suffering embodiment. He gave her hope by stating: "Thy desire shall be to thy husband, and he shall rule over thee." It had already been promised that Lucifer would one day be conquered by the "seed" of Eve (if not by Eve herself, according to some versions). And here she is told: "Thy desire shall be to thy husband," Adam. Why? Because under the law of sowing and reaping, it was Adam and Eve–no one else–who would be required to repair the breach they had caused for themselves and others, both reconciling themselves and all humanity to God, and providing healing for the spiritual diseases accruing from aeons of estrangement from Him. Eve was to long for the "seed" which would reverse their submission to Lucifer by crushing his "head"–that is, by annihilating his dominance over the human race–or for the chance to do so herself. Who would this "seed" be? Adam, "thy husband," revealed in his perfection as Jesus of Nazareth, the Savior.

And so the plan was this: Adam and Eve would have to struggle upward, slowly, painfully, through countless lives, experiencing the bitterness of constant birth and death. At long, long last they would regain Paradise, take up once more the bodies ("garments") of light they had there discarded, and from there on evolve upward through all the realms of subtle creation, until at last, the final barrier broken, they were to merge with God: Adam with the Son-Father and Eve with the Holy Spirit-Mother. (This is because, as we have already said, each spirit as it is breathed forth from the transcendent Father is polarized to the divine archetypes of either the Son [Male] or the Holy Spirit [Female], and spends the majority of its evolution in bodies of corresponding polarities.)

> In times of old Adam tripped and fell, bruised,
> Disappointed of the hope of becoming divine;
> But, made godlike by the union of the Word, he rises,
> Acquires through the Passion freedom from passion
> And is glorified: the Son Who sits upon the throne
> With the Father and the Spirit.

This hymn (of the Byzantine Octoechos, Tone One, Matins Canon to the Cross and the Resurrection) is sung every two months in the Sunday morning services of the Eastern Orthodox Churches of the Byzantine Rite. The same idea is given by the prophet Micah when predicting the birth of Christ, "the One to be ruler in Israel, Whose goings forth have been from of old, from everlasting" (Micah 5:2). (The Septuagint reads: "His goings forth were from the beginning, from the days of the age," indicating that his rebirths, his goings forth, had been occurring from the first of this creation cycle or age [aeon].)

The debt and the payment

From this exalted status, a spirit normally would take the final step of passing into the transcendent Being of the Father, shedding even their subtle polarization, and thus completing the cycle. "And he shall go no more out" (Revelation 3:12) unless he wills to do so. But not so for Adam and Eve. Their cosmic debt–a debt to all humanity–necessitated their turning back from the final glory and, in their total identity with the Son and the Mother, descending to earth as incarnations of the Son and the Mother, working redemption for all, and thereby fulfilling the divine requirement. "For since by man came death, by man came also the resurrection of the dead. For as in Adam all die, even so in Christ shall all be made alive.... The first man Adam was made a living soul; the last Adam was made a quickening spirit.... The first man is of the earth, earthy: the second man is the Lord from heaven. As is the earthy, such are they also that are earthy: and as is the heavenly, such are they also that are heavenly. And as we have borne the image of the earthy, we shall also bear the image of the heavenly" (I Corinthians 15:21, 22, 45,47-49).

This is not just the Christian view, but the Jewish doctrine as well. The *Nishmath Chaim*, a writing contemporary with Jesus and the Apostles, says: "The sages of truth remark that [the name] Adam contains the initial letters of Adam, David, and Messiah; for after Adam sinned, his spirit passed into David, and the latter having also sinned, it passed into the Messiah" (Folio 152, column 2). Let us look at how this was accomplished and its present-day meaning for us.

Since she was first in falling, Eve–no longer a separated spirit, but herself the Mother through perfect union– descended to earth and incarnated as the daughter of Saints Joachim and Anna. Joachim and Anna had grown old without having children. Yet, when he was serving in Jerusalem as high priest, Saint Joachim was told by an angel that he would indeed have a child. Further, the angel told him to go to a particular gate of Jerusalem, and there he would meet Saint Anna, who had also received the same revelation and instruction. And it was so–the two met right at the gate.

The priests of the temple knew of the angelic prophecy and arranged for its fulfillment. Taking Saints Joachim and Anna, they separated them and led them to different parts of the temple. Though few knew it, there was a passage under the temple which ran directly beneath the Holy of Holies where the Ark of the Covenant was kept. The Ark was the one object on earth where God's presence dwelt in its fullness, and in the Ark was the golden jar of manna. The Ark and the golden jar were prophetic symbols of the Virgin Mary, for the Divine Presence was to overshadow her so Jesus–her son and Son of God–the new manna, the "bread from heaven" (John 6:51), would be conceived and dwell within her until his birth.

At the divinely-ordained hour, Saints Joachim and Anna were taken to opposite ends of the passage, unknown to each other. The priests simply instructed them to start walking forward into the passage, and then left.

The conception and birth of Mary

The holy ones did as they were told. Meeting directly beneath the Most Holy Place, in a state of divine exaltation the two saints embraced in greeting. Brilliant light descended from the Ark above and enveloped them both, and in that moment Anna conceived the glorious Virgin, not through the earthly mode of sexual intercourse, but in the way Adam and Eve would have channeled the upward-moving spirits into Paradise had they not fallen. Thus the Virgin was conceived in the truly human manner of Paradise.

Returning home, Saints Joachim and Anna awaited the birth on earth that would be the beginning of restoration. At the appointed time, friends of Saint Anna came to assist her in what they all assumed would be a normal birth. But when the time came for the Virgin's full entrance into this world, Saint Anna shone with such light that she could not be seen by her friends. Lifted up from the earth, she found in her arms the child, which had miraculously passed from within her directly to her arms without any labor pains whatsoever. Slowly the light diminished, and she descended to the earth. By inspiration, she placed the child upon the ground, who stretched forth her legs, stood for a moment, and then took three steps–not the unsteady toddling of a child, but the assured walk of an adult. Instantly, Saint Anna caught her up and vowed that this child's feet would never again touch the earth until she was presented before the Lord in Jerusalem as a virgin of the Temple.

Three years passed, during which the sacred Mary lived in the interior of her parents' house, never once stepping out upon the earth or even going into the outer rooms of the house.

Mary's presentation and life in the Temple

At the end of three years Saints Joachim and Anna took their divine child to Jerusalem to offer her unto the Lord's service as one of the consecrated virgins who dwelt in the Temple and made the priestly vestments and the great veil which hung before the Holy of Holies. To demonstrate to the priests that, though so young, the child came of her own will and understanding, the two saints decided to place her at the foot of the seven flights of steps which ascended to the Temple, and to have her walk up them unassisted. However, when they placed her upon the earth for the first time since her birth, she was instantly transported to the top of the steps!

In that exact moment, by prophetic inspiration Saint Zachariah, the future father of Saint John the Baptist, who was high priest at that time, came forth with all the Temple virgins, who were dressed in festal garb and holding lighted lamps as for a wedding. They surrounded Mary, who began to dance in their midst. Moving slowly while she continued to dance, they led her into the Temple. Not once did she glance back to Saints Joachim and Anna, but kept her gaze intently toward the Holy Place where none but the priests were allowed to go, and which no woman had even seen, much less entered.

To the astonishment of all, Saint Zachariah led the Virgin into the Holy Place. With furious indignation, the priests pursued them to take her from there. But upon entering they saw to their compounding chagrin that Saint Zachariah was leading her into the Holy of Holies, where they themselves could not go, only the High Priest being allowed to enter–and that only once in each year.

In this manner the new Ark of the New Covenant was witnessed to by the holy Zachariah. (He was later killed by the soldiers of Herod at the instigation of some of the priests, who felt that he had defiled the Temple by these actions.) There is speculation that upon the entrance of the New Ark into the Most Holy Place, the Old Ark was taken away by the angels to an unknown place.

Thenceforth the Virgin lived in the Temple, working in silence and prayer. Until the day of her entry, she had eaten no food but the milk of Saint Anna. Here she was fed exclusively on the food of Paradise which was brought to her by angels. This was to ensure that her body would be capable of enduring the mighty power that would descend at the incarnation of Christ in her womb. An "earthy" body would have been destroyed, just as was Uzza's when he simply touched the Ark whereon the Presence rested Which was to dwell within her for nine months (I Chronicles 13:7-10). Moreover, her body had to be of the type from which Adam-Christ could draw a suitable physical vehicle for his redemptive work.

The weaving of the veil for the Most Holy Place was a great honor, bestowed on the virgins by the drawing of lots. The most honored part of this task was the weaving of the purple–the color symbolizing the Divine Presence–into the veil. While she lived in the Temple, the lots always assigned to Mary the task of weaving the purple into the veil. This was indicative of the fact that she was going to provide Christ–the Messiah–with the veil of flesh by which he would enshroud his incarnate glory, revealing it only to Peter, James, and John at his Transfiguration (Matthew 17:1-9).

The espousal of Mary

It was the custom that upon reaching a suitable age the Temple virgins should become espoused, and later married. To marry a Temple virgin was considered one of the highest honors in Israel. Ordinarily the families of the virgins made the arrangements, but in the case of the wondrous Virgin, the priests decided that they would themselves determine which man should marry her, for they knew she was unique.

The prophets among them were given the revelation that all the eligible men of Israel who were descended from

David should come to Jerusalem, bringing their staffs; and the one whose staff was seen to bear flowers would be the one to whom the Virgin should be betrothed.

This was announced, and the men assembled in the Temple. After prayers were offered, it was seen that no staff had flowered. The priests were confused at this, but when it was reported to them that one man had not brought his staff, the priests demanded that he be brought to them. There came before them a venerable, elderly man: Joseph, a carpenter from Nazareth. He explained that in his haste to reach the Temple that morning he had left his staff behind and, feeling assured that he could never be chosen for such an honor (also, having secretly made a vow of virginity in his youth), he had not felt the need to return and fetch it. The priests commanded him to bring his staff without delay. He did so, and in the presence of all, during the prayers of the priests his staff blossomed with lilies–symbols of virginity. In this way, the priests knew that he was to be espoused to the Virgin, and made all arrangements.

After the espousals (she was never married), the Virgin went with Saint Joseph to Nazareth. There the saint had already divided his house into two completely separate dwellings–one for the Virgin and the other for himself. For by the budding of the lilies he knew that God still honored his vow of virginity, and that the Virgin should dwell with no mortal, however holy he might be.

Then: "When the fullness of the time was come, God sent forth his Son, made of a woman, made under the law, To redeem them that were under the law, that we might receive the adoption of sons" (Galatians 4:4-5).

The beginning of redemption

"In the sixth month the angel Gabriel was sent from God unto a city of Galilee, named Nazareth, To a virgin espoused to a man whose name was Joseph, of the house of David; and the virgin's name was Mary" (Luke 1:26, 27).

"Mary" [Miriam] comes from a Hebrew root word, *meriy*, which means disobedient, rebellious. It also means bitterness. So by her name we know that this Virgin was the one who anciently disobeyed God, who rebelled against His prohibition of the tree of knowledge, and thus brought great bitterness to herself and all the world. But this was "the fullness of time." She had won her crown of life; she had been enthroned. No longer mortal, to the eyes of the spirit she was "clothed with the sun, and the moon under her feet, and upon her head a crown of twelve stars" (Revelation 12:1). Yet, the ancient debt had to be paid. What was sown must not only be reaped, it must

be counteracted. She had returned to restore. Lucifer had planned for her to be the mother of demons, but she was instead to be the Mother of Christ the new Adam, and thereby truly "the Mother of all the living" (Genesis 3:20).

It was not Lucifer, cunningly bearing death in his words, who now came to her. No, it was Gabriel, "The Mighty Man of God," who drew near, not in the Paradise of delight, but on suffering earth, to the most despised town of Israel, whose name, however, meant "shining place of fruitfulness," a name surely given it by prophetic inspiration.

"And the angel came in unto her, and said, Hail, thou that art highly favoured, the Lord is with thee: blessed art thou among women. And when she saw him, she was troubled at his saying, and cast in her mind what manner of salutation this should be" (Luke 1:28-29). Caution and humility–at what a terrible price had those lessons been learned well by her! With the fullness of consciousness, she remembered perfectly the seduction in Paradise–and by an archangel. It was wisdom and not desire that now ruled in her spirit, and she would no more be deceived by promises of glory and power.

"And the angel said unto her, Fear not, Mary: for thou hast found favour with God. And, behold, thou shalt conceive in thy womb, and bring forth a son, and shalt call his name Jesus. He shall be great, and shall be called the Son of the Highest: and the Lord God shall give unto him the throne of his father David: And he shall reign over the house of Jacob for ever; and of his kingdom there shall be no end" (Luke 1:30-33).

At last the prophetic directive of God was being fulfilled: "Thy desire shall be to thy husband, and he shall rule over thee" (Genesis 3:16). Adam now was coming as King, a Son of God, a Deliverer of bound spirits.

It was revealed to the holy stigmatist Anna Catharine Emmerich (1774-1824), that from her earliest childhood the holy Virgin had fervently prayed for the Messiah to appear in her days, and petitioned continually that she might be permitted to become a handmaid to the mother of the Messiah. The desire to serve now counterbalanced that fatal yearning to "be as God." But her eagerness for his coming did not cancel her awareness that holiness alone adorns the abode of God. Still fearing beguilement, "Mary [said] unto the angel, How shall this be, seeing I know not a man?" (Luke 1:34). For she knew full well God's intention that "a virgin shall conceive, and bear a son, and shall call his name Immanuel" (Isaiah 7:14). Even more: she did not demand to know for herself, as she once did in Paradise, but, though cautious, was willing to be instructed in humility by a messenger of God.

"And the angel answered and said unto her, The Holy Ghost shall come upon thee, and the power of the Highest shall overshadow thee: therefore also that holy thing which shall be born of thee shall be called the Son of God. And, behold, thy cousin Elisabeth, she hath also conceived a son in her old age: and this is the sixth month with her, who was called barren. For with God nothing shall be impossible" (Luke 1:35-37).

Then was she convinced. Just as she had descended in Light from the Most Holy Place in Jerusalem and was conceived by Saint Anna, so also Jesus, the Son, was to descend and be conceived by her. The archangel's reference to Elizabeth, her cousin, further told her that he knew the mode of her own conception–a secret hidden from Lucifer and his agents. His words were further proof to her in these two ways: (1) they showed that the archangel shared the secrets of God; and (2) if further doubt remained in her mind, she could verify his words by a visit and consultation with the righteous Elizabeth.

Now she reversed her ancient disobedience by uttering the words that mystics have told us the entire host of heaven drew near in anxiety and hope to hear: "Behold the handmaid of the Lord; be it unto me according to thy word" (Luke 1:38). No longer aspiring to an imitation of divinity, she, having attained a truly divine status, knew herself to be a servant of the Highest.

Eve reverses the ancient wrong

"And he shall rule over thee" (Genesis 3:16). What did the Daughter of David accomplish in this? She compensated for the greed and prideful ambition she had indulged in Paradise "when the woman saw that the tree was good for food, and that it was pleasant to the eyes, and a tree to be desired to make one wise, [and] she took of the fruit thereof, and did eat, and gave also unto her husband with her; and he did eat" (Genesis 3:6). For now she was offered, not an exaltation to divinity and enjoyment, but the bitterness and humiliation of bearing a child out of wedlock and thereby incurring the stigma of fornication–a stigma immeasurably increased because she had been a virgin of the Temple. Betrayal of both the priests of the Temple and of the just Joseph would also be imputed to her shame. And if she dared tell the truth– that the conception was divine–blasphemy punishable by death would also be laid to her charge. Throughout the course of history, unbelievers, some of them even bearing the name of Christian, would snigger and sneer, mocking her "pretence." She, the spotless virgin, would bear the label of adulteress throughout millennia.

In Paradise, disobediently she stretched forth her hands for selfish enjoyment and power. Now, in obedience she stretched forth her hands for mockery and shame. There in Paradise Lucifer assured her that she would not die, but now she willingly faced that risk–for stoning was the punishment of adultery–to fulfill the will of God. This is why she has been given the title "Queen of Martyrs," for in her heart she did indeed lay down her life, and in the following years silently endured the mockery and reproach of those around her. Even when her sacred body was being borne to the tomb, a man attempted to upset the bier and throw her body to the ground, shouting that she was an adulteress and a blasphemer. In life and death she accepted shame and so remedied her ancient pride.

In Paradise, heeding the words of a fallen archangel, she had offered the death-bearing fruit to Adam, and in consequence we all die. But in Nazareth, having believed the message of a faithful archangel, she offered to Adam—now Son of God and Messiah—the fruit of her womb: a Body through which we could be enabled to live.

Through her disobedience in Paradise, Eve lost the light garment and became "naked." On this day in Galilee she became enrobed in the Overshadowing Light. By eating the fruit in Paradise she worked our banishment therefrom; and now, by abstaining all her life from earthly food and living solely on the food of Paradise, she effected our restoration thereto. There she hid in shame from God to hide her nakedness, but now she who wove the veil to enshroud His Presence in the Temple cried: "Behold the handmaid of the Lord!"

So began the payment of the final installment of the primal Debt. As Saint Roman Melodos wrote in his hymn on the Annunciation:

> Adam was thrust out; that is why God devised the renewal for

Adam and had him come forth from thy womb.

A woman formerly cast him down, and now a woman raises him up–

A virgin from a virgin.

Adam begins reversing the ancient wrong

And Adam our father–what did he do in this vein? He also accepted the medicament of humiliation. By being born of Mary he would hear the reproach: "We be not born of fornication" (John 8:41), and the further accusation: "Say we not well that thou art a Samaritan?" (John 8:48)–that is, that he was illegitimate, his father being a Samaritan. Even now, those who think themselves sophisticated enjoy chuckling over the "myth" of the Virgin Birth. But the equivalent of the Nazareth reversal took place thirty years after his conception there. Coming to the Jordan, he was baptized with the baptism of repentance, that he might "fulfill all righteousness" (Matthew 3:15).

"And Jesus, when he was baptized, went up straightway out of the water: and, lo, the heavens were opened unto him, and he saw the Spirit of God descending like a dove, and lighting upon him" (Matthew 3:16). Having publicly expressed humble obedience at the hand of one whom he had plunged into the abyss of death through disobedience, he, like Mary, was enrobed in the Overshadowing. And the voice which he hid from in Paradise as it called: "Where art thou?" then sounded "from heaven, saying, This is my beloved Son, in whom I am well pleased" (Matthew 3:17).

In the wilderness

More remained to be accomplished and so "immediately the Spirit driveth him into the wilderness" (Mark 1:12). He Who was driven from Paradise was now driven into the barren places where he would repair the destruction he had long ago wrought.

"And when he had fasted forty days and forty nights, he was afterward an hungred" (Matthew 4:2). In Paradise he had known no hunger, yet had eaten of the fruit in deliberate, conscious rebellion. He had been assured there of immortality, but now faced the death of the body through hunger. There he had a companion to persuade him to transgress and upon whom he might later cast the blame. ("And the man said, The woman whom thou gavest to be with me, she gave me of the tree, and I did eat." Genesis 3:12.) Now he found himself in solitude. Alone he faced the coming ordeal. And come it did: Lucifer, once again. He who came gliding into Paradise on feet of deceit, now after aeons drew near again. As on

that day in Nazareth, the hosts of heaven were looking on in prayerful anxiety. In that moment all could be forfeit.

Eve had at least the excuse that the guile of Lucifer had deceived her. "And the Lord God said unto the woman, What is this that thou hast done? And the woman said, The serpent beguiled me, and I did eat." Genesis 3:13). Adam had no such rationalization, for Lucifer spoke not to him. Because of this, Eve-Mary could reverse her actions in speaking with a holy Archangel. But her son would not be so exempted.

Lucifer came for the great test: Had Adam truly escaped thoroughly from his dominion? Was he now so evolved that the very possibility of Lucifer's influence had been abrogated? If a single flaw remained, he would fall again. This was fully known to him, to Lucifer and to the angelic hosts.

"And when the tempter came to him, he said, If thou be the Son of God, command that these stones be made bread" (Matthew 4:3). Lucifer had heard that Adam whom he had subverted in the Garden and turned into an instrument of his will had now appeared on the earth plane, after aeons. This was no surprise to him, for was he not the one who had guaranteed the continuous return of spirits? But rumor on the human, angelic and demonic planes had it that Adam was no more a bound man, but a Son of God, Whose name, Jesus, meant "God shall save," and that he had descended to earth "that he might destroy the works of the devil" (I John 3:8).

Of course, Lucifer did not believe it, but he knew well that "with God all things are possible" (Matthew 19:26), though he also knew that he does all things according to exact laws. Yet, God had been quiet the last century or so, and the prophecies of a Messiah who might turn out to be more than a political leader had been around for a long time. And Elijah, now appearing as John the Baptizer (see Matthew 11:13-14; 17:10-13), had practically worshipped this Jesus. Some among the humans claimed that a voice from heaven called Jesus "My Beloved Son" when he was baptized by John. If people were even thinking such things then Lucifer must challenge it.

And so he did: "If thou be the Son of God, command that these stones be made bread." In response to the first half of the challenge, Jesus would either say he was not a Son of God, like a reasonable fellow, or he would say he was, and then Lucifer would have some real fun with his pawn from Paradise. If he gave no reply at all, but did turn the stones into bread, Lucifer would have uncovered in him three major delusions: (1) the delusion that food gives life, (2) the delusion that life is of the body; and (3) the desire to wield spiritual power for personal satisfaction.

"But he answered and said, It is written, Man shall not live by bread alone, but by every word that proceedeth out of the mouth of God" (Matthew 4:4). In Paradise he had yearned to "be like God," refusing to admit his status as an evolving spirit far from the divine condition. Now, having truly attained to godhood, yet being clothed in a mortal body, he acknowledged the limitation necessity had imposed upon him and, though Son of God, humbly called himself man, professing total dependence on his Father. But was this profession sincere? If so, the ancient deceiver knew how to bend even that to his cunning.

"Then the devil taketh him up into the holy city, and setteth him on a pinnacle of the temple, And saith unto him, If thou be the Son of God, cast thyself down: for it is written, He shall give his angels charge concerning thee: and in their hands they shall bear thee up, lest at any time thou dash thy foot against a stone" (Matthew 4:5-6). Lucifer's insulting words were calculated to evoke any of his prideful ways that might have remained buried in the heart of Jesus. Even more, he had brought Jesus to the holiest place on earth, the place where God's power would surely be demonstrated–where one might feel the most confident in putting divine favor to the test. But he had no idea that Jesus knew quite well that "If I bear witness of myself, my witness is not true" (John 5:31). Not only did Jesus have this knowledge, his consciousness had been utterly transformed since those fatal moments in Paradise. Then, when his highest aspiration should have been to be an humble servant of God, he had instead sought not to serve but to "be like God." Now, "in him dwelleth all the fullness of the Godhead bodily" (Colossians 2:9), and having attained to the divine knowledge he had vainly reached for under the tutelage of Lucifer, he had "made himself of no reputation, and took upon him the form of a servant" (Philippians 2:7). Therefore: "Jesus said unto him, It is written again, Thou shalt not tempt the Lord thy God" (Matthew 4:7). Only God is egoless enough to be disinterested in "proving" himself. Thus, Lucifer had cause for worry.

We must realize that Jesus was not being at all "tempted" in the sense of being inwardly drawn or tantalized to commit evil or folly and having to exert will power to resist these urgings. He was being tested (which is a more accurate translation of the Greek term *peirazo*) by Lucifer to determine if he had indeed totally escaped from his (Lucifer's) taint and power. For only a "lamb without blemish" could reverse Lucifer's accomplishments and "take away the sins of the world," freeing it from his false bondage. As I have said, if one spot, one mote, of Lucifer's "image" had remained in Christ, he would have failed the test.

But Lucifer had more. "Again, the devil taketh him up into an exceeding high mountain, and sheweth him all the kingdoms of the world, and the glory of them; And saith unto him, All these things will I give thee, if thou wilt fall down and worship me" (Matthew 8:8-9). The primal desire of Lucifer had been for the rulership of the lower world, including this earth plane. He had attempted to make over Adam and Eve into his image by promising them the power that knowledge would theoretically bring them. He was also utilizing the basic drive implanted in them by the true God–the impulse to "increase in wisdom and stature" unto the attainment of divinity with its plenitude of knowledge and power. Lucifer, having no real power of his own–no, not even to influence others–has to corrupt, to bend the natural impulses bestowed on us by God. Therefore his strategy is ever to divert into negative channels the natural, divine powers of the spirit. It is the power of God alone which Lucifer usurps in his rebellion.

Saint Luke, in his account of our Lord's testing by Lucifer, adds some additional material: "And the devil, taking him up into an high mountain, shewed unto him all the kingdoms of the world in a moment of time. And the devil said unto him, All this power will I give thee, and the glory of them: for that is delivered unto me; and to whomsoever I will I give it. If thou therefore wilt worship me, all shall be thine" (Luke 4:5-7). What a bitter dose were the words: "for that is delivered unto me." By whom had it been delivered to him? *By the very one he was now testing!*

We know from the teachings of the Scriptures and the saints that all of us must one day behold with devastating clarity the results of all our deeds. Here, the Lord Jesus saw what his act of disobedience had wrought, compounding evil throughout countless ages. Although the panorama might be attributed to the malice of Lucifer, in actuality the fundamental responsibility was his own. He beheld what he had brought upon humanity. No longer could he blame Eve or God. The truth was displayed before him. Now, in that moment of trial, he alone must turn back the flood he had released so long ago. It was his own handiwork that Lucifer offered him, a prize that aeons ago he would have seized in avid folly. But it was not the earth and its kingdoms which Jesus desired. He willed to win Paradise and the higher kingdoms–not for himself, but for all beings entrapped by Lucifer through his former cooperation.

Lucifer could not even imagine the attainment of Christ. To him, as to us, egoless merging in the greater Being of God was to "lose individuality," to "become a nothing," to cease to "be." But Jesus had not the mind of Lucifer, he had the mind of Christ–of Christhood itself. There was no possibility of his cooperating with Lucifer now, so: "Then saith Jesus unto him, Get thee hence, Satan: for it is written, Thou shalt worship the Lord thy God, and him only shalt thou serve" (Matthew 4:10). For Jesus, there could be no longer the serving of either himself or another besides God. He had not only rejected the will of Lucifer, but also any separate, conflicting will he might have, surrendering all to God– his true Self.

"Then the devil leaveth him, and, behold, angels came and ministered unto him" (Matthew 4:11). So Jesus conquered, not through power or knowledge–both of which Lucifer himself possessed to a great, though perverted, degree–but through humility, a weapon Lucifer cannot withstand when wielded in even the slightest degree, for it exists not at all in his armoire of shadows. Even in his replies to Lucifer, Christ embodied humility. For though from his own vast attainments he could without impunity speak "of himself," he yet only quoted the words of the holy scriptures, not presuming any authority of his own, although "all power in heaven and on earth" was his (Matthew 28:18). Lucifer had encountered this divine quality once before–in his conqueror, Michael the Great Archon, who, though armored with the power of God, yet simply said: "The Lord rebuke thee" (Jude 9).

All victories entail the winning of something. What did Christ win for us on that day? We will find the answer in his words to the Apostles on the night of his betrayal: "Be of good cheer; I have overcome the world" (John 16:33). The bondage to the wheel of birth and death which had kept us whirling perpetually in the orbit of this earth, unable to break free and pass on to higher evolution, had now been broken. For the power the earth had over our minds, keeping us oriented to ceaseless return, was wiped out. But, like the pair in the Fifteenth Arcanum of the Tarot, we must throw off the illusion of bondage and live our freedom.

> Awake thou that sleepest,
> And arise from the dead,
> And Christ shall give thee light.
> (Ephesians 5:14)

Gethsemane and Paradise

Much had thus been done in the work of restoration, but more yet remained. The Garden of Paradise had to be wrestled for in the Garden of Gethsemane.

"Then cometh Jesus with them unto a place called Gethsemane, and saith unto the disciples, Sit ye here, while I go and pray yonder. And he took with him Peter and the two sons of Zebedee, and began to be sorrowful and very heavy. Then saith he unto them, My soul is exceeding sorrowful, even unto death: tarry ye here, and watch with me. And he went a little further, and fell on his face, and prayed, saying, O my Father, if it be possible, let this cup pass from me: nevertheless not as I will, but as thou wilt" (Matthew 26:36-39)

In Paradise there was a tree, the partaking of which at the command of God would give knowledge, but the partaking of which in disobedience would bring death–not just to Adam, but to all the spirits beneath him. He took, he ate, he brought death upon us all. Now he faced another tree: the Cross. It was not "pleasant to the eyes, a tree desirable".... He ate of the fruit in full awareness. So now, too, he was fully aware of the Cross. And in that hour he had to break the illusory, desperate clinging to physical embodiment which bound us all to rebirth. He had to destroy forever the instinctive delusion that physical life is the true Life. And it was not to be easy.

"And he cometh unto the disciples, and findeth them asleep, and saith unto Peter, What, could ye not watch with me one hour? Watch and pray, that ye enter not into temptation: the spirit indeed is willing, but the flesh is weak" (Matthew 26:40-41).

In Paradise he blamed his companion Eve for his transgression. In Gethsemane he was therefore alone–no one stood with him. He alone was responsible for his action in Paradise, and he had to be alone now, for it was his debt he was struggling to repay. It was a result of his action that "the flesh is weak." He there reaped in knowledge what he had sown in ignorance. His words of surrender to the divine will were indeed right and noble, but what was required was more than rhetoric–and had not yet been achieved. And so:

"He went away again the second time, and prayed, saying, O my Father, if this cup may not pass away from me, except I drink it, thy will be done. And he came and found them asleep again: for their eyes were heavy. And he left them, and went away again, and prayed the third time, saying the same words" (Matthew 26:42-44). It is not easy to undo what has so heedlessly been done! But this third time he approached the end.

"And there appeared an angel unto him from heaven, strengthening him. And being in an agony he prayed more earnestly: and his sweat was as it were great drops of blood falling down to the ground. And when he rose up from prayer, and was come to his disciples, he found them sleeping for sorrow." (Luke 22:43-45).

The final steps

He went forth to the final stage of the necessary restoration. He who desired knowledge and power was now bound as though helpless (John 18:12). He was in mockery asked to display his prophetic knowledge (Matthew 26:67-68) and tortured (Matthew 27:27-30). Herod demanded miracles of power (Luke 23:8); Pilate cynically asked for philosophical definitions (John 18:38). He was weak and foolish in the eyes of all (Matthew 27:35-44). He whose folly enslaved us all was betrayed for thirty pieces of silver—the price of a slave (Matthew 26:14-15).

Standing on Pilate's balcony, he saw how completely man's mind had been polarized to love evil, for the crowd chose to receive among themselves the murderer Barabbas, and rejected him who wished to save them. He was spared nothing in the drinking of the Cup. How ironic it must have been to his spirit when he heard the shouted words: "We have a law, and by our law he ought to die, because he made himself the Son of God" (John 19:17). He fulfilled all that was needful, refusing even the drink offered to dull the pain of crucifixion. "And they gave him to drink wine mingled with myrrh: but he received it not" (Mark 15:23).

The pair who transgressed in Paradise were reunited on Golgotha for the final steps of reconciliation. She, "the woman" who "saw that the tree was good for food, and that it was pleasant to the eyes, and…took of the fruit thereof, and did eat" (Genesis 3:6), there beheld another "tree," the Tree of the Cross. It was her own son she saw hanging there as the "fruit," and the sword pierced through her soul, as had been prophesied (Luke 2:35). With what fullness of meaning did Jesus deliver these words to the whole race of men: "Behold thy mother" (John 19:27).

Plunged into the abyss of the illusion of separation from God, drinking the dregs of the utter desolation it inevitably produces, and undergoing the experience of death we all so fear, though it is the gateway to true existence in God, he completed the cycle of divine justice and could say: "It is finished" (John 19:30).

Descending triumphant into hades, he went unto those spirits who had been bound in darkness from the days when they had mocked and ignored him in his incarnation as Noah, thereby bringing death upon themselves (I Pet. 3:18-20). Those he both instructed and released that they might continue their evolution through further births.

Further, he came unto those righteous spirits who had evolved beyond the necessity for rebirth on this material plane but were caught in a spiritual limbo,

being unable to enter Paradise and continue their upward growth to God. Raising them up, in a true "resurrection from the dead," he brought them into Paradise and set them free.

Worthy is the Lamb that was slain
To receive power, and riches, and wisdom,
And strength and honor, and glory, and blessing!
(Revelation 5:12).

Amen.

God and Man?

In many statements in the Bible we find a clear indication that Jesus Christ of Nazareth was both God and Man, but we must understand that in a very precise manner–vastly different from that of "orthodox" Christianity. Jesus was god-man because he was deified humanity–a man that had transcended humanity and entered into divine being. He continually referred to himself as "the son of man," to indicate that he had originated from the earth and had taken birth many times as a human being in his striving upward to become a Son of God. And since nothing is ever lost when we enter the plenitude of God, he still remained a Son of Man just as much as he thenceforth was a Son of God. This is a great mystery, but it is a mystery of Truth.

So when, as the Nicene Creed says, "for us men and for our salvation" he "came down from heaven," he was careful to make a definite distinction between his immortal nature as God and his earthly appearance as Jesus of Nazareth, a man originally subject to the laws of birth and death, but who by those very laws had conquered them, transcended them, and opened the way to ultimate freedom. When we see how the great mystery-drama of salvation unfolds–especially the fact that Adam and Eve had to work the restoration of a humanity they had plunged into the hopelessness of a distorted material plane existence–it becomes clear as to how Jesus is the Savior of all mankind, even though the majority of the world has never at any time been Christian.

Moreover, when we understand that in this creation cycle Jesus and Mary are the First (Original) Parents of the human race returned to redeem it, we can understand how it is that they strike a chord of kinship in every nation and every religion on earth. It is this subliminal recognition of our primeval father and mother, and the spiritual freeing which they wrought, that causes Buddhists to consider Christ a buddha or a bodhisattva, Hindus to believe in him as an avatara, a divine incarnation, and Jews and Moslems to look upon him as a great prophet. There is more wisdom than usually supposed in the Christmas song, *Some Children See Him*, in which Christ is described in the ways children of varying cultures, races, and religions throughout the world "see" him. No figure in world religions evokes this universal sympathy and feeling of intimacy–despite the evil example of degenerate Christianity with its crusades and missionarying based on the derogation of other faiths. Wiser than us, they have been able to distinguish between Christ and false churchianity.

But this insight comes from the intimate relationship we all share with him who has caused both our death and our resurrection. "For as in Adam all die, even so in Christ shall all be made alive" (I Corinthians 15:22). *All shall be made alive.* Christ has ensured this, just as by his ancient disobedience "sin entered the world, and death through sin, and thus death spread to all men" (Romans 5:12). He, by the primal law of sowing and reaping, doing and undoing, of necessity undid his former error, thus opening the path to salvation to all, without exception. Not one spirit can ever be eternally damned. Just as no one escaped the effect of Adam's disobedience, so no one shall be unaffected by his restoration. The innermost consciousness of all knows this.

Attaining divinity

There are passages in the New Testament that definitely indicate the view of Christ as having attained to his divine status.

In Acts 13:33 and Hebrews 1:5 and 5:5, the Apostles apply to Christ the Psalm verse: "Thou art My Son; this day have I begotten Thee" (Psalms 2:7). Those teachers known as Fathers of the Church have told us with extreme emphasis that the Only-Begotten of the Father, the Son, the Second Person of the Holy Trinity, has been such from eternity, that the "begetting" of the Son is a purely symbolic term for the mysterious, perpetual process within the Godhead Itself–a process that takes places in eternity, never in time. Therefore, the use of the expression "this day" indicates an event within the time-cycle of relative existence, spoken to someone who in the past was not a Son of God, but then by divine fiat has become a Son of God. Applied to Christ Jesus, it plainly shows that he attained the status of sonship– of union and identity with the eternal Person of the Godhead known as the Son–that he experienced the transmutation from limited consciousness into limitless Divine Consciousness, in which he could be said to be "begotten" by the Father himself. And it happened at a particular time–after aeons of upward evolution.

In Philippians, we find two more of those verses that seem puzzling to those who do not have a full understanding of Jesus' past and mission. "[Jesus], being in the form of God, thought it not robbery to be equal with God: Wherefore God also hath highly exalted him, and given him a name which is above every name" (Phil. 2:6, 9). These two verses clearly outline that Jesus did not think it wrong to aspire to divinity, and that he had indeed gained it by being made so ("exalted") by God, Who called him "Son."

Further evidence is in the Gospel of John. Speaking with Nicodemus, Jesus told him: "No man hath ascended up to heaven, but he that came down from heaven, even the Son of man which is in heaven." (John 3:13). With these words, he indicates that he had previously "ascended" to heaven–a symbolic term for the state of divine being–before "descending" to earth as a Son of Man to save it. If he had always been in that state, he would not have said that he had ascended to it beforehand.

Errors regarding Jesus

Because implied–though often unadmitted–dualism has led Western and Eastern Christian thinking astray for most centuries, we almost insist instinctively in viewing God and man as mutually exclusive and contradictory rather than as one, which they are. God is in man, and man is in God. Where there is one there must of necessity be the other. The existence of God and man is One.

Through ignorance of this truth there have been three major errors about our Lord Jesus Christ:
1. That he is only a man, not God;
2. That he is only God;
3. That in him were really two persons–a man and God.

All three are erroneous and even harmful, because they deny our capability of ascending to our divine destiny. If Jesus was only a man, then it is not possible to be one with God through him. If Jesus was only God, then he has not fully touched and reconciled us men unto union with God as Saint Paul affirms in II Corinthians 5:18-19. In the Bible, "reconciliation" does not mean that God was angry with us "sinners" and had to be appeased or placated by Christ. Rather, it means that in our distorted state brought about by the fall of Adam and Eve we were estranged from our own true self and God. But Adam-Jesus by ascending to godhood and then descending to us opened for us the way to return to our original state as undistorted images of God so we would no longer be in contradiction to the divine life and being. On the other hand, if there were two persons in Christ Jesus, the capacity for union in the sense of perfect identity would be abrogated and the irrevocable duality and separation of God and man affirmed.

By this we see that the Christological controversies which took up so much of early Church history were not at all the word-jugglings they are superficially assumed to be. Rather, they were of the essence, because the nature of Christ is our nature, and the attainment of his likeness is our salvation. So the definition of Christ is also the definition of the perfected Christian. Unless we understand the what and why of his incarnation we can have no idea of our true goal in Christian life.

Crucifixion and atonement

Jesus' incarnation and crucifixion was for the expiation of his personal karmic debt–not to God, but to that segment of humanity in this creation cycle that had been affected by his past negative actions and influence as explained previously. Yet all humanity has been benefitted by his incarnation to different degrees and in different ways to some extent. However the exoteric Christian view of the meaning and purpose of the crucifixion, especially the aspect of "atonement, is profoundly mistaken and misses completely the true nature of the crucifixion in the divine plane of restoration. For the crucifixion accomplished a profound change in the earth itself and thereby the entire human race.

Creation–universal manifestation, actually–occurs in cycles which the Bhagavad Gita speaks of as "days" and "nights." (See the section on chapter eight, verses sixteen to nineteen, in *The Bhagavad Gita For Awakening*.) At the beginning of a creation cycle the cosmos and the evolving intelligences within it are exactly as they were at the end of the previous cycle. It is a continuous process.

As explained earlier (but repeated here so what I am saying will be in context) somewhere in the previous creation cycles there occurred a tremendous and traumatic event when one of the seven Prajapatis or Lords of Creation was so deluded as to attempt to wrest the part of creation over which he had supervision from the will and control of God (Ishwara). Many spirits that assisted him joined with him in the rebellion and both he and they were cast out and down from their former positions in the creative order. Because the name of a person has a powerful link with them, the names of this rebel and his followers have not been revealed. In the Bible they are simply referred to as "Lucifer" and his angels, that are now in the state of demons. They are in constant war against the divine order.

Every planet has a guide and guardian archangel who supervises the evolution of the sentient beings on that planet. The archangel of our planet was involved in the Luciferic rebellion, and when he was unseated and banished from the earth, humanity and all other sentient beings were without their guide and guardian. How long and throughout how many creation cycles this condition prevailed is not known, but part of Jesus' mission was to correct this situation and begin the restoration of earth and humanity–a process that is just beginning and will require untold time for its completion. His very birth two thousand years ago was the beginning, and his crucifixion was the complete empowerment and initiation. As he said in Revelation: "Behold, I have set before thee an open door, and no man can shut it" (3:8). The process will doubtless be slow, perhaps even encompassing more than one creation cycle, but it will be sure. It is in this sense that Jesus is "the savior of the world," not according to the dogmas of exoteric Christianity.

The restoration of the earth and humanity took place in three steps: the crucifixion, death and resurrection of Jesus.

The first step involved the shedding of his blood. Everything we think of as solid matter is really vibrating consciousness, and that included blood. The Japanese philosopher and healer, Mokichi Okada, often said that blood is congealed spirit. This is why the Bible equates blood with life itself: it is spirit in manifestation. (See Genesis 9:4; Leviticus 17:11, 14; and Deuteronomy 12:23.) The human race has been aware of this from time beyond calculation. This is why bloodline has always been important in both religion and society. When something is so ingrained as to be inherent in our nature we say it is "in the blood."

Being a liberated being, Jesus was a manifestation of divine consciousness. His body and blood were consciousness fully awakened. The Sanskrit term *chinmaya*–formed of consciousness–applies here. Therefore, when Jesus' blood flowed down upon the earth at the crucifixion, and especially after his heart was pierced by the lance, his consciousness became united with the earth and the earth became united with his consciousness. At that point many things happened, but one of the most important was the ending of the earth's "orphaned" status. For Jesus himself became the guard and guide of the earth and all therein, sentient and insentient. This involved the reuniting of the earth with the solar world and the flooding of the earth with the solar energies of awakening and evolution. The spiritual darkness of the earth was ended. It was "baptized" in Jesus blood. Not in the gross material sense, but in the highest spiritual sense of union with divinity. This was the erasure of "sin" and the "curse" of both Lucifer's and Adam's falls. (See also Appendix One: The Life-giving Mystery of Golgotha

The second step was Jesus' conscious and willful departure from his body. "And when Jesus had cried with a loud voice, he said, Father, into thy hands I commend my spirit: and having said thus, he gave up the ghost" (Luke 23:46). Leaving his body, "he went and preached unto the spirits in prison; which sometime were disobedient, when once the longsuffering of God waited in the days of Noah, while the ark was a preparing, wherein few, that is, eight souls were saved by water" (I Peter 3:19-20). As mentioned before, these people had refused his warning in his incarnation as Noah, yet he had a deep bond with them which enabled him then to deliver them from their spiritual "bottleneck" and enable them to continue onward in their evolution in this and higher worlds.

The third step was his resurrection. Through his body, pure consciousness that it was, Jesus was linked to every human being on the earth. When he rose from the dead he opened many avenues that had been closed to human beings as an effect of the Luciferian rebellion. Simply being citizens of the earth doomed them to this situation. But more, he infused into them and their descendants potentials for a degree of consciousness and spiritual

76

attainment which humanity had not possessed before. The true New Age began the moment his spirit and deified subtle bodies united with his resurrected physical body and began a transmutation hitherto unknown for many creation cycles. And this is still continuing and will keep on even in future cycles.

Now none of this has anything to do with "believing in Jesus" or being a Christian, as exoteric Christianity insists–if they believed in what I have described, which they do not. It is all about eternally being a divine spirit, a god within God. It is universal in scope and not limited to any religion or philosophy. But it is why subliminally people throughout the world feel a kinship with Jesus despite the ravages of ignorant Churchianity. In every religion there are those who intuit their connection with Jesus. They often say: "Jesus was one of us." A very holy Buddhist monk once visited our monastery and told us that one time in India a Christian missionary demanded of him: "Do you believe in Jesus as your savior?" "Yes," he answered and then asked the missionary: "Do you believe in Buddha as your savior" "No!" shouted the missionary. "Well, then," the monk said, smiling, "you have only one savior, but I have two!"

What this means to us

The true Gospel–Good News–of Christ is the knowledge that we can all ascend to God, as he confirms in Revelation 3:21: "To him that overcometh will I grant to sit with me in my throne, even as I also overcame, and am set down with my Father in his throne." Here again we see the clear demonstration that the Lord Jesus himself journeyed on the path that we, too, now tread; that his attainment is our hope. This is why he said to Saint Mary Magdalene: "Go to my brethren, and say unto them, I ascend unto my Father, and your Father; and to my God, and your God" (John 20:17). We see this further in Psalm 110:1: "The Lord said unto my Lord, Sit thou at my right hand,...." In Luke 20:42, Jesus applies this to himself, and Saint Peter applies it to him in Acts 2:34, having previously stated that Jesus had been "by the right hand of God exalted, and having received of the Father the promise of the Holy Ghost..." (Acts 2:33). Saint Peter also says later on in Acts: "Him hath God exalted with his right hand to be a Prince and a Savior" (Acts 5:31). The author of the book of Hebrews (1:13) also applies the above Psalm verse to Jesus. He further applies to Jesus the verse from II Samuel: "I will be his father, and he shall be my son" (II Sam. 7:14). The implications are obvious. Does this mean that Jesus is not God? No.

It means that Jesus absolutely is God, but like all of us he had to ascend to that status. His case is unique in that he (and the Virgin) had to turn back from the final Union and descend to earth to repair the damage they had done in previous ages.

Even now you and I are divine sons of God, potentially. This is why Saint John wrote: "Beloved, now are we the sons of God, and it doth not yet appear what we shall be: but we know that, when he shall appear, we shall be like him; for we shall see him as he is. And every man that hath this hope in him purifieth himself, even as he is pure" (I John 3:2-3). In this passage Saint John outlines several amazing spiritual facts: (1) we are ourselves already–eternally–sons of God; (2) we yet have to attain to a full revelation and conscious taking on of that status which (3) is to be the same as that of Christ Jesus; to which end we must (4) purify ourselves, attaining a purity identical with his.

Originally all that is written here was known to all Christians. Therefore Saint Paul could write to the Corinthians: "My speech and my preaching was…in demonstration of the Spirit and of power: That your faith should not stand in the wisdom of men, but in the power of God. Howbeit we speak wisdom among them that are perfect:…the wisdom of God in a mystery, even the hidden wisdom, which God ordained before the world unto our glory:…as it is written, Eye hath not seen, nor ear heard, neither have entered into the heart of man, the things which God hath prepared for them that love him. But God hath revealed them unto us by his Spirit: for the Spirit searcheth all things, yea, the deep things of God.… [And] we have the mind of Christ" (I Corinthians 2:4-7, 9-10, 16). And: "Let a man so account of us, as of the ministers of Christ, and stewards of the mysteries of God" (I Corinthians 4:1). (For an exposition of these deifying Mysteries see *The Yoga of the Sacraments*.)

The knowers of these Mysteries, by faithful application, "with open face beholding as in a glass the glory of the Lord, are changed into the same image from glory to glory, even as by the Spirit of the Lord" (II Corinthians 3:18). "And as we have borne the image of the earthy, we shall also bear the image of the heavenly.… Behold, I shew you a mystery; We shall not all sleep, but we shall all be changed, For this corruptible must put on incorruption, and this mortal must put on immortality. So when this corruptible shall have put on incorruption, and this mortal shall have put on immortality, then shall be brought to pass the saying that is written, Death is swallowed up in victory. O death, where is thy sting? O grave, where is thy victory?" (I Corinthians 15:49, 51, 53-55).

Then we shall not only know the meaning of, but shall ourselves be living embodiments of his further words: "For as in Adam all die, even so in Christ shall all be made alive. ...when he shall have delivered up the kingdom to God, even the Father; when he shall have put down all rule and all authority and power. The last enemy that shall be destroyed is death. And when all things shall be subdued unto him, then shall the Son also himself be subject unto him that put all things under him, that God may be all in all" (I Corinthians 15:22, 24, 26, 28).

And then all cosmology is ended, for the cosmos, like the evolving spirits within it, shall have returned to the Bosom of the Father, the All In All. Then to each one shall be fulfilled the promise spoken to Saint John: "He that overcometh shall inherit all things; and I will be his God, and he shall be my son" (Revelation 21:7).

Appendix One

The Life-giving Mystery of Golgotha

For two thousand years much has been said about "the cleansing blood" of Jesus as the only means of redemption and salvation. Over the centuries this has become distorted into superstition, nonsense and blasphemy under the aegis of "orthodoxy" in Christianity. But it does have a glorious meaning undreamed of by those who pride themselves on their self-proclaimed orthodoxy.

Evolution is the Universal Law, yet even laws can be thwarted by the evil and the ignorant and produce stagnation and even reversal of their evolutionary journey. Through the "fall of man" brought about by Lucifer, evolution on the earth was reduced to this chaotic state. After many ages, Adam who was responsible along with Lucifer for this condition, had evolved to absolute perfection through all the worlds, ascending the ladder of cosmic evolution to total attainment of his divine potential: a Christ.

Adam-Jesus then returned to earth to begin the reversal of the terrible condition produced by his transgression in Paradise and compounded through the ages by his human descendants and the Luciferian spirits (fallen angels). He did this by merging his divine Life and Consciousness with the earth itself and those human beings who desired and were capable of drawing on that life and taking the long, blessed path he had trodden to their own eventual Christhood–even though it might take many rebirths on the earth.

He accomplished this salvific union in two ways: by his incarnation in a human body through the Virgin Mary and by his crucifixion. By the first he united his defied nature with human nature and by the second he united his awakened divine consciousness with the very earth itself.

In the Old Testament we find statements that the life and the blood are one, that the blood is the vehicle (body) of the life: the spirit. The Japanese philosopher and healer, Mokichi Okada, simply said: "Blood is congealed spirit." The blood of each human being comes exclusively from the father, which is why his children are considered to be of his family and bear the name of his father's family. But

Jesus had no human father, so where did his blood come from? It was a purely supernatural entity, a manifestation of the Holy Spirit Who overshadowed the Virgin Mary and brought about his conception. ("And the angel answered and said unto her, The Holy Ghost shall come upon thee, and the power of the Highest shall overshadow thee: therefore also that holy thing which shall be born of thee shall be called the Son of God." Luke 1:35)

Therefore, when Jesus was crucified and his blood flowed into the earth, it became united with him and in this way he assumed the office and relationship with the earth that the Archangel Lucifer had been given at its creation. From thenceforth Jesus was the Guide and Guardian of the earth in all its aspects, including all the life forms living in and upon it, especially the human race of whom he already was the father since he had been Adam.

The life of Christ and the life of the earth became one. And the evolution of the individual human being became part of that Christ life. This is why spiritually awakened people throughout the world, no matter what their nationality or religion might be, feel a kinship with Jesus and a reverence for and faith in him. But most important, the impulse of the spirit to return to its Source, to enter into conscious, full union with God, can freely arise in them. This does not mean they have to be or become Christians–that would no doubt be a hindrance to them because Churchianity has almost totally displaced true Christianity. (See *The Christ of India*.)

Just as God can be worshipped in all religions, so Jesus the Christ, the illumined and perfected Son of God, has meaning for all who seek contact with God, whatever their religion may be. Just as God is greater than all religion, so is Christ Jesus in his true being. And his intention for all humanity is that they all be consciously one with God just as he is one with God. Without this perspective, it is impossible to understand Jesus or his purpose for being born on earth by his divine will.

Only with the foregoing facts in mind can we then comprehend the real meaning of his words as recorded by Saint John in the seventeenth chapter of his Gospel: "These words spake Jesus, and lifted up his eyes to heaven, and said, Father, the hour is come; glorify thy Son, that thy Son also may glorify thee: As thou hast given him power over all flesh, that he should give eternal life to as many as thou hast given him. And all mine are thine, and thine are mine; and I am glorified in them. That they all may be one; as thou, Father, art in me, and I in thee, that they also may be one in us" (John 17:1-2, 10, 21).

APPENDIX TWO

This is a section from my book, The Christ of India, *which I recommend you obtain and read for a fuller understanding of the Who and Why of Jesus.*

Who was–and is–Jesus?

In Vedic religion it is believed that the human race had more than one set of foreparents. It appears from the accounts given in Genesis that the inhabitants of the Mesopatamian and Mediterranean areas as well as those regions to their north were the descendants of Adam and Eve. These are the very people that, without exception, became Christians in the first centuries after Christ. The reason is evident: their profound ancestral link to Jesus.

The *Nishmath Chaim* (Fol. 152, col. 2), a book contemporary with Jesus and the Apostles which would have been studied by Saint Paul, says: "The sages of truth remark that Adam contains the initial letters of Adam,

David, and Messiah; for after Adam sinned his soul passed into David, and the latter having also sinned, it passed into the Messiah."

He who was Jesus of Nazareth was Adam. When Adam "fell," he was in Paradise, the astral plane immediately above the physical creation. But the alteration in consciousness which resulted from his transgression rendered him unable to function in that subtle world, so he sank back down into the physical plane, through which he had already evolved before entering Paradise. In Genesis we read: "And for Adam and his wife the Lord God made tunics of skin, and clothed them" (Genesis 4:21). Although many now take this to mean that they were given clothes like the cavemen are depicted wearing, Christians originally understood that the real meaning of this verse was that God created physical bodies—the human organism—for Adam and Eve to inhabit, and thus they continued in the cycle of life, death, and rebirth upon the earth.

The Old Testament is the account of Adam's evolving to become the Christ. Adam evolved through life after life as Noah, Abraham, Joseph, Moses, David, Elisha, and Isaiah. Ascending to and evolving beyond higher and higher worlds, at last he passed through the final barrier of the angelic (seraphic) planes and attained perfect union with the Father/Son aspect of God. From this point the soul normally passes into total union with the pure, transcendent Being of the Father, ending the evolutionary cycle, but it was not so for Adam. He was in debt: a debt owed to all of his descendants, one of such magnitude that it could only be paid by one of infinite consciousness–which Adam now was.

So Adam returned, of necessity, to our earth plane in his earthly incarnation as Jesus of Nazareth, the Christ (Messiah)–not only paying the debt, but showing and opening the way to the Father for his children, many of whom were, through rebirth, by that time scattered throughout the earth.

When Jesus told his apostles to make disciples among all nations he was not meaning that the whole world was to be converted to Christianity, but that they should seek out those who in past lives had been his descendants and been negatively affected by the fall of Adam. He was referring to them when he had told them: "Other sheep I have, which are not of this fold [of Israel]: them also I must bring, and they shall hear my voice; and there shall be one fold, and one shepherd" (John 10:16). He did not mean that the entire human race was to become Christian.

When Saint Paul speaks of Jesus as being the "second man [Adam]…from heaven" (I Corinthians 15:47), he speaks quite literally, and not figuratively. He also speaks literally about Adam paying his debt: "For since by man came death, by man came also the resurrection of the dead. For as in Adam all die, even so in Christ shall all be made alive" (I Corinthians 15:21, 22). Does this mean, then, that Jesus is only a man, and not the Son of God? No. Jesus positively *is* the Son of God. And so shall we all be Sons of God like him. But first he was a man–one of the foreparents of the human race, as we have said. Then he ascended to divinity, attaining perfect union with God.

The real good news (which is what "gospel" means) is that as Adam passed from fallen ignorance and sin unto perfect Divinity, so shall his disciples do the same through him. Jesus affirmed this when he told the Apostles: "Be of good cheer; *I have overcome the world*" (John 16:33). Later, to his Beloved Apostle John, he said: "To him that overcometh will I grant to sit with me in my throne, *even as I also overcame,* and am set down with my Father in his throne" (Revelation 3:21). As it was with Jesus, so shall it be with us. The passage from humanity to divinity–to Christhood–is the real essence of Saint Thomas Christian belief. The life of the Lord Jesus as given in the four Gospels is also a symbolic mystery-drama showing how the soul of each person becomes a Christ–an anointed of the Lord.

Again, we are saying that Jesus the Christ was *once* a human being just like us, but is now in the status of Son of God, just as we shall be. Saint John wrote: "Beloved, now are we the sons of God, and it doth not yet appear what we shall be: but we know that, when he shall appear, we shall be like him; for we shall see him as he is" (I John 3:2). That is, when we "see" God (the Father) through union with him, we shall be perfectly transmuted into his image and likeness and thus truly become the sons of God, hearing the words: "Thou art my Son; this day have I begotten thee" (Psalms 2:7, Acts 13:33, Hebrews 1:5, 5:5) in mystic vision. This is the very thing that happened to Adam/Jesus, which is why he is called "the first-fruits of them that slept" (I Corinthians 15:20).

APPENDIX THREE

*The Past and Future
Lives of Jesus Christ*

The following is an outline of the major incarnations of Jesus as related in the Bible. However, considering the nature of the ascent of the jivatman to the full realization of the Paramatman, there may have been many more rebirths on the earth of the person we call Jesus, and of course many in the astral and causal worlds as he evolved to divinity.

Adam

This has been considered at some length in this book, so there is nothing more to add.

Noah

When the human race was in danger of extinction from flood (and most religions, including Hinduism have accounts of the flood), Noah built the ark to save many of his (as Adam) descendants, but no one would pay attention, so only Noah and his wife and their children were saved. Thus Noah became the forefather of those who repopulated the earth.

Abraham

When he was Abraham things began moving toward his advent of as the Messiah and a universal savior. From then onward his incarnations were as his own descendants.

The most significant aspect of his incarnation as Abraham was his ancestry, for Abraham's ancestors were those of the Yadava Clan of India to which Krishna belonged. Shortly after Krishna's departure from this world, the entire Yadava Clan disappeared from India. The reason for this is not known, but they settled in the area of Mesopotamia, taking with them their religious observances as Shaivites, worshippers of Shiva. (See *The Christ of India*.) This is of great significance, for Jesus as a descendant of Abraham was of the same bloodline as Krishna, and his ancestral religion was the religion of India: Sanatana Dharma. So when he went to India, he was literally returning to his roots, both physically and spiritually.

Joseph

As Joseph he was the salvation of the Hebrew descendants of his great-grandfather Abraham, when as a powerful member of the Egyptian nation he enabled the Hebrews to take refuge from devastating famine by emigrating to Egypt. His visions indicated that he would be born as the Messiah.

Moses

After living some time in Egypt, the Hebrews became the slaves of the Egyptians and endured great suffering and faced extinction as a distinct people. The daughter of the Pharaoh adopted the Jewish baby she rescued from the Nile and named him Moses. Since he was not of the royal bloodline he could not become Pharaoh, but he was raised in the palace and trained to become the head of the Egyptian religion (the traditional office of the second sons of the Pharaohs). But turning from that honor he chose to identify with the Hebrews and in time led them out of Egypt toward their former home in Israel, giving them the Law from God on Sinai by which they would be prepared for the incarnation of the Messiah.

In some liturgical hymns of both the (traditional) Roman Catholic and Eastern Orthodox Churches, Moses and Jesus are identified as the same person. This is very striking in the Roman Catholic Good Friday "Reproaches" (*Popule meus*). Similar references are scattered at random throughout the Eastern Orthodox hymns for the various major feasts of the year.

David

As already pointed out in the main text, the Jewish tradition is that the Messiah will be the reincarnation of both Adam and David. David opened a new era in the history of Israel and established the Ark of the Covenant on Mount Zion. The Psalms of David have been the official prayer book and hymnal of both Judaism and Christianity, and contain prophecies of the Messiah, especially regarding the crucifixion in Psalm 21/22.

Elisha

Jesus said openly that Saint John the Baptist was the reincarnation of Elijah (Matthew 11:14; 17:10-13; Mark 9:13). Jesus was the reincarnation of Elijah's disciple, Elisha, who also was a major influence in the Jewish religion.

Isaiah

As Isaiah, he who was to be Jesus became known as the Messianic Prophet because of his many prophecies regarding (himself as) the Messiah.

Jesus (Piscean Age)

There is no need for me to outline the life of Jesus after his birth at the beginning of the Piscean Age, except to point out that Saint Peter in his epistle (I Peter 3:18-20) says that after leaving his body at the crucifixion, Jesus entered the astral world and delivered from a kind of astral prison the souls there that had rejected his teachings as Noah and as a consequence had drowned in the flood.

More information on the life of Jesus that is not commonly known is to be found in my book, *The Unknown Lives of Jesus and Mary*, and *The Aquarian Gospel* by Levi Dowling

Future appearance in the Aquarian Age

In the esoteric tradition of Judaism it is said that the Messiah would be born twice: once as the son of Joseph and be rejected, and again as the son of David and be accepted as the Messiah. This second appearance will occur in the Aquarian Age which began in the year 2000, the preparation for which began at the time of the great stellium in Aquarius in 1962.

No predictions are given for this incarnation except his recognition by the Jewish people, but it is my opinion that he will reconcile and unite the descendants of Abraham, the Jews and the Arabs. And, considering their present state of consciousness and belief, I think we can assume that he will be denounced as Antichrist by the exoteric Christians.

The past and future lives of the Virgin Mary

The past of the Virgin as Eve, the Mother of the human race in this creation cycle, has been covered.

As the wife of Noah, she became the mother of those descended from her children who populated the earth after the flood.

She was Miriam, the sister of Moses and Aaron and a prophetess. She is written about in the fifteenth chapter of Exodus and the twelfth chapter of Numbers. Her death is mentioned in Numbers 20:1.

She was Sarah, the wife of Abraham, and was also of the Yadava clan. As such she was the foremother of the Jewish nation and deeply revered throughout the centuries.

She was Bathsheba, the wife of David and mother of Solomon.

She was Deborah, and as one of the judges of Israel guided the spiritual life of Israel.

She was Hannah, the mother of Samuel who would anoint and proclaim David as the king of Israel.

She was Judith, the great heroine of Israel, both prophetess and judge. An entire book of the Bible was written about her which is found only in Roman Catholic and Eastern Orthodox Bibles.

Finally she was Mary, the daughter of Joachim and Anna, the divinely conceived and virgin mother of Jesus, the "great wonder in heaven; a woman clothed with the sun, and the moon under her feet, and upon her head a crown of twelve stars" (Revelation 12:1), Co-Redemptress of the world, of whom God had prophesied in Paradise, telling Lucifer: "I will put enmities between thee and the woman, and thy seed and her seed: she shall crush thy head, and thou shalt lie in wait for her heel" (Genesis 3:15). Just as she gave birth to Jesus, so she gave birth to the Church on Pentecost when through her the Holy Spirit was given to the Apostles. And in this way she is the spiritual Mother of all Christians.

APPENDIX FOUR

Introduction to Soham Yoga

I–The Practice of Soham Yoga Meditation

1) Sit upright, comfortable and relaxed, with your hands on your knees or thighs or resting, one on the other, in your lap.

2) Turn your eyes slightly downward and close them gently. This removes visual distractions and reduces your brain-wave activity by about seventy-five percent, thus helping to calm the mind. During meditation your eyes may move upward and downward naturally of their own accord. This is as it should be when it happens spontaneously. But start out with them turned slightly downward without any strain.

3) Be aware of your breath naturally (automatically) flowing in and out. Your mouth should be closed so that

all breathing is done through the nose. This also aids in quieting the mind. Though your mouth is closed, the jaw muscles should be relaxed so the upper and lower teeth are not clenched or touching one another, but parted. Breathe naturally, spontaneously. Your breathing should always be easeful and natural, not deliberate or artificial.

4) Then in a very quiet and gentle manner begin *mentally* intoning Soham in time with your breathing. (Remember: Soham is pronounced like our English words *So* and *Hum*.)

Intone *Soooooo*, prolonging a single intonation throughout each inhalation, and *Huuummm*, prolonging a single intonation throughout each exhalation, "singing" the syllables on a single note.

There is no need to pull or push the mind. Let your relaxed attention sink into and get absorbed in the mental sound of your inner intonings of Soham.

Fit the intonations to the breath–not the breath to the intonations. If the breath is short, then the intonation should be short. If the breath is long, then the intonation should be long. It does not matter if the inhalations and exhalations are not of equal length. Whatever is natural and spontaneous is what is right.

Your intonation of *Soooooo* should begin when your inhalation begins, and *Huuummm* should begin when your exhalation begins. In this way your intonations should be virtually continuous, that is:

SooooooHuuummmSoooooooHuuummmmSoooooooHuuummmm.

Do not torture yourself about this—basically continuous is good enough.

5) For the rest of your meditation time keep on intoning Soham in time with your breath, calmly listening to the mental sound.

6) In Soham meditation we do not deliberately concentrate on any particular point of the body such as the third eye, as we want the subtle energies of Soham to be free to manifest themselves as is best at the moment. However, as you meditate you may become aware of one or more areas of your brain or body at different times. This is all right when such sensations come and go spontaneously, but keep centered on your intonations of Soham in time with your breath.

7) In time your inner mental intonations of Soham may change to a more mellow or softer form, even to an inner whispering that is almost silent, but the syllables are always fully present and effective. Your intonations may even become silent, like a soundless mouthing of Soham or just the thought or movement of Soham, yet you will still be intoning Soham in your intention. And of this be sure: *Soham never ceases.* Never. You may find that your

intonations of Soham move back and forth from more objective to more subtle and back to more objective. Just intone in the manner that is natural at the moment.

8) In the same way you will find that your breath will also become more subtle and refined, and slow down. Sometimes the breath may not be perceived as movement of the lungs, but just as the subtle pranic energy movement which causes the physical breath. Your breath can even become so light that it seems as though you are not breathing at all, just *thinking* the breath (or almost so).

9) Thoughts, impressions, memories, inner sensations, and suchlike may also arise during meditation. Be calmly aware of all these things in a detached and objective manner, but keep your attention centered in your intonations of Soham in time with your breath. Do not let your attention become centered on or caught up in any inner or outer phenomena. Be calmly aware of all these things in a detached and objective manner. They are part of the transforming work of Soham, and are perfectly all right, but keep your attention centered in your intonations of Soham in time with your breath. Even though something feels very right or good when it occurs, it should not be forced or hung on to. The sum and substance of it all is this: It is not the experience we

are after, but the effect. Also, since we are all different, no one can say exactly what a person's experiences in meditation are going to be like.

10) Soham japa and meditation can make us aware of the subtle levels of our being, many of which are out of phase with one another and are either confused or reversed in their polarity. The japa and meditation correct these things, but sometimes, especially at the beginning of meditation, we can experience these aberrations as uncomfortable or uneasy sensations, a feeling or heaviness or stasis or other peculiar sensations that are generally uncomfortable and somehow feel "not right." When this occurs, do not try to interfere with it or "make it better." Rather, just relax, keep on with the japa/meditation, calmly aware and let it be as it is. In time the problem in the subtle energy levels will be corrected and the feeling will become easy and pleasant. Simple as the practice is, it has deep and far-reaching effects, as you will see for yourself.

11) If you find yourself getting restless, distracted, fuzzy, anxious or tense in any degree, just take a deep breath and let it out fully, feeling that you are releasing and breathing out all tensions, and continue as before.

12) Remember: Soham Yoga meditation basically consists of four things: a) sitting with the eyes closed;

b) being aware of our breath as it moves in and out; c) mentally intoning Soham in time with the breath; and d) listening to those mental intonations: all in a relaxed and easeful manner, without strain.

Breath and sound are the two major spiritual powers possessed by us, so they are combined for Soham Yoga practice. It is very natural to intone Soham in time with the breathing. It is simple and easy.

13) At the end of your meditation time, keep on intoning Soham in time with your breath as you go about your various activities, listening to the inner mantric sound, just as in meditation. One of the cardinal virtues of Soham sadhana is its capacity to be practiced throughout the day. The *Yoga Rasyanam* in verse 303 says: "Before and after the regular [meditation] practice, the repetition of Soham should be continuously done [in time with the breath] while walking, sitting or even sleeping…. This leads to ultimate success."

Can it be that simple and easy? Yes, because it goes directly to the root of our bondage which is a single–and therefore simple–thing: loss of awareness. Soham is the seed (bija) mantra of nirvanic consciousness. You take a seed, put it in the soil, water it and the sun does the rest. You plant the seed of Soham in your inner consciousness through japa and meditation and both your Self and the

Supreme Self do the rest. By intentionally intoning *So* and *Ham* with the breath we are linking the conscious with superconscious mind, bringing the superconscious onto the conscious level and merging them until they become one. This is what the Bhagavad Gita (6:29) means by the term yoga-yukta–joined to yoga. It is divinely simple!

The secret of success is regularity in meditation. "A diamond is a piece of coal that never gave up." If you meditate regularly, every day, great will be the result. Water, though the softest substance known, can wear through the hardest stone by means of a steady dripping. In the old story of the tortoise and the hare, the tortoise won the race because he kept at it steadily, whereas the hare ran in spurts. He ran much faster then the tortoise, but the irregularity of his running made him lose the race. Meditation keeps moving onward in its effect when regularly practiced, producing steady growth through steady practice. The more we walk the farther we travel; the more we meditate the nearer and quicker we draw to the goal.

The four elements of Soham Yoga meditation

There are four components of Soham Yoga meditation:
1) sitting with closed eyes;

2) being aware of the breath as it moves in and out;

3) mentally intoning Soham in time with the breathing;

4) listening to the inner, mental intonations of Soham and becoming absorbed in the subtle sound.

These are the essential ingredients of Soham Yoga meditation, and we should confine our attention to them. If in meditation we feel unsure as to whether things are going right, we need only check to see if these four things are being done and our attention is centered in them. If so, all is well. If not, it is a simple matter to return to them and make everything right. Success in Soham Yoga consists of going deeper and deeper into the subtle sound of the Soham mantra as we intone it within. It is the thread leading us into the center of Reality.

Gorakhnath summed up his Soham Yoga practice and its effect in this manner: "The mind is the root and the breath is the branch; the sound [of Soham] is the guru and attention [to the sound] is the disciple. With the essence called deliverance [*nirvana tattwa*–the principle of liberation] Gorakhnath wanders about, himself in himself" (Gorakh Bodha 10).

Invariables

There are certain invariables of Soham Yoga meditation.

1) We always meditate with closed mouth and eyes.

2) We always mentally intone Soham in time with the breath.

3) Our mental intonations of Soham, like the breath to which we are linking them, should be virtually continuous, not with long breaks between them. That is: *SoooooHuuummmSoooooHuuummmSoooooHuuummm* (Basically continuous is good enough.)

4) The inner, mental, intonations of Soham never cease. Never. We must not let passivity or heaviness of mind interrupt our intonations by pulling us into negative silence. That would be a descent rather than an ascent.

5) The focus, the center of attention, of our meditation is the sound of our mental intonations of Soham in time with our breath. In an easeful and relaxed manner we become absorbed in that inner sound.

6) Our mental intonations of Soham are gentle, quiet and subtle.

For more information on Soham Yoga, visit our website:

OCOY.ORG

ABOUT THE AUTHOR

Swami Nirmalananda Giri (Abbot George Burke) is the founder and director of the Light of the Spirit Monastery (Atma Jyoti Ashram) in Cedar Crest, New Mexico, USA.

In his many pilgrimages to India, he had the opportunity of meeting some of India's greatest spiritual figures, including Swami Sivananda of Rishikesh and Anandamayi Ma. During his first trip to India he was made a member of the ancient Swami Order by Swami Vidyananda Giri, a direct disciple of Paramhansa Yogananda, who had himself been given sannyas by the Shankaracharya of Puri, Jagadguru Bharati Krishna Tirtha.

In the United States he also encountered various Christian saints, including Saint John Maximovich of San Francisco and Saint Philaret Voznesensky of New York.

For many years Swami Nirmalananda has researched the identity of Jesus Christ and his teachings with India and Sanatana Dharma, including Yoga. It is his conclusion that Jesus lived in India for most of his life, and was a yogi and Sanatana Dharma missionary to the West. After his resurrection he returned to India and lived the rest of his life in the Himalayas.

He has written extensively on these and other topics, many of which are posted at OCOY.org.

ATMA JYOTI ASHRAM
(LIGHT OF THE SPIRIT MONASTERY)

Atma Jyoti Ashram (Light of the Spirit Monastery) is a monastic community for those men who seek direct experience of the Spirit through yoga meditation, traditional yogic discipline, Sanatana Dharma and the life of the sannyasi in the tradition of the Order of Shankara. Our lineage is in the Giri branch of the Order.

The public outreach of the monastery is through its website, OCOY.org (Original Christianity and Original Yoga). There you will find many articles on Original Christianity and Original Yoga, including *The Christ of India*. *Foundations of Yoga* and *How to Be a Yogi* are practical guides for anyone seriously interested in living the Yoga Life.

You will also discover many other articles on leading an effective spiritual life, including *Soham Yoga: The Yoga of the Self* and *Spiritual Benefits of a Vegetarian Diet*, as well as the "Dharma for Awakening" series—in-depth commentaries on these spiritual classics: the Bhagavad Gita, the Upanishads, the Dhammapada, the Tao Teh King and more.

You can listen to podcasts by Swami Nirmalananda on meditation, the Yoga Life, and remarkable spiritual people he has met in India and elsewhere, at http://ocoy.org/podcasts/

You can watch over 100 videos on these topics and more, including recordings of online satsangs where Swami Nirmalananda answers various questions on practical aspects of spiritual life.

Visit our Youtube channel here:
Youtube.com/@lightofthespirit

Reading for Awakening

Light of the Spirit Press presents books on spiritual wisdom and Original Christianity and Original Yoga. From our "Dharma for Awakening" series (practical commentaries on the world's scriptures) to books on how to meditate and live a successful spiritual life, you will find books that are informative, helpful, and even entertaining.

Light of the Spirit Press is the publishing house of Light of the Spirit Monastery (Atma Jyoti Ashram) in Cedar Crest, New Mexico, USA. Our books feature the writings of the founder and director of the monastery, Swami Nirmalananda Giri (Abbot George Burke) which are also found on the monastery's website, OCOY.org.

We invite you to explore our publications in the following pages.

Find out more about our publications at
lightofthespiritpress.com

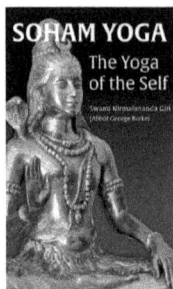

Soham Yoga
The Yoga of the Self

A complete and in-depth guide to effective meditation and the life that supports it, this important book explains with clarity and insight what real yoga is, and why and how to practice Soham Yoga meditation.

Discovered centuries ago by the Nath yogis, this simple and classic approach to self-realization has no "secrets," requires no "initiation," and is easily accessible to the serious modern yogi.

Includes helpful, practical advice on leading an effective spiritual life and many Illuminating quotes on Soham from Indian scriptures and great yogis.

"This book is a complete spiritual path." –Arnold Van Wie

Light of Soham
The Life and Teachings of Sri Gajanana Maharaj of Nashik

Gajanan Murlidhar Gupte, later known as Gajanana Maharaj, led an unassuming life, to all appearances a normal unmarried man of contemporary society. Crediting his personal transformation to the practice of the Soham mantra, he freely shared this practice with a small number of disciples, whom he simply called his friends. Strictly avoiding the trap of gurudom, he insisted that his friends be self-reliant and not be dependent on him for their spiritual progress. Yet he was uniquely able to assist them in their inner development.

The Inspired Wisdom of Gajanana Maharaj
A Practical Commentary on Leading an Effectual Spiritual Life

Presents the teachings and sayings of the great twentieth-century Soham yogi Gajanana Maharaj, with a commentary by Swami Nirmalananda.

The author writes: "In reading about Gajanana Maharaj I encountered a holy personality that eclipsed all others for me. In his words I found a unique wisdom that altered my perspective on what yoga, yogis, and gurus should be.

"But I realized that through no fault of their own, many Western readers need a clarification and expansion of Maharaj's meaning to get the right understanding of his words. This commentary is meant to help my friends who, like me have found his words 'a light in the darkness.'"

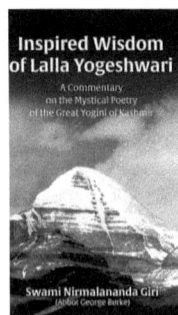

Inspired Wisdom of Lalla Yogeshwari
*A Commentary on the Mystical Poetry
of the Great Yogini of Kashmir*

Lalla Yogeshwari was a great fourteenth-century yogini and wandering ascetic of Kashmir, whose mystic poetry were the earliest compositions in the Kashmiri language. She was in the tradition of the Nath Yogi Sampradaya whose meditation practice is that of Soham Sadhana: the joining of the mental repetition of Soham Mantra with the natural breath.

Swami Nirmalananda's commentary mines the treasures of Lalleshwari's mystic poems and presents his reflections in an easily intelligible fashion for those wishing to put these priceless teachings on the path of yogic self-transformation into practice.

Dwelling in the Mirror

A Study of Illusions Produced By Delusive Meditation
And How to Be Free from Them

Swami Nirmalananda says of this book:

"Over and over people have mistaken trivial and pathological conditions for enlightenment, written books, given seminars and gained a devoted following.

"Most of these unfortunate people were completely unreachable with reason. Yet there are those who can have an experience and realize that it really cannot be real, but a vagary of their mind. Some may not understand that on their own, but can be shown by others the truth about it. For them and those that may one day be in danger of meditation-produced delusions I have written this brief study."

BOOKS ON YOGA & SPIRITUAL LIFE

Satsang with the Abbot

Questions and Answers about Life, Spiritual Liberty,
and the Pursuit of Ultimate Happiness

The questions in this book range from the most sublime to the most practical. "How can I attain samadhi?" "I am married with children. How can I lead a spiritual life?" "What is Self-realization?" "How important is belief in karma and reincarnation?"

In Swami Nirmalananda's replies to these questions the reader will discover common sense, helpful information, and a guiding light for their journey through and beyond the forest of cliches, contradictions, and confusion of yoga, Hinduism, Christianity, and metaphysical thought.

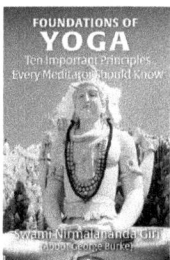

Foundations of Yoga

Ten Important Principles Every Meditator Should Know

An introduction to the important foundation principles of Patanjali's Yoga: Yama and Niyama

Yama and Niyama are often called the Ten Commandments of Yoga, but they have nothing to do with the ideas of sin and virtue or good and evil as dictated by some cosmic potentate. Rather they are determined by a thoroughly practical, pragmatic basis: that which strengthens and facilitates our yoga practice should be observed and that which weakens or hinders it should be avoided.

Yoga: Science of the Absolute

A Commentary on the Yoga Sutras of Patanjali

The Yoga Sutras of Patanjali is the most authoritative text on Yoga as a practice. It is also known as the Yoga Darshana because it is the fundamental text of Yoga as a philosophy.

In this commentary, Swami Nirmalananda draws on the age-long tradition regarding this essential text, including the commentaries of Vyasa and Shankara, the most highly regarded writers on Indian philosophy and practice, as well as I. K. Taimni and other authoritative commentators, and adds his own ideas based on half a century of study and practice. Serious students of yoga will find this an essential addition to their spiritual studies.

The Benefits of Brahmacharya
A Collection of Writings About the Spiritual,
Mental, and Physical Benefits of Continence

"Brahmacharya is the basis for morality. It is the basis for eternal life. It is a spring flower that exhales immortality from its petals." Swami Sivananda

This collection of articles from a variety of authorities including Mahatma Gandhi, Sri Ramakrishna, Swami Vivekananda, Swamis Sivananda and Chidananda of the Divine Life Society, Swami Nirmalananda, and medical experts, presents many facets of brahmacharya and will prove of immense value to all who wish to grow spiritually.

Living the Yoga Life
Perspectives on Yoga

"Dive deep; otherwise you cannot get the gems at the bottom of the ocean. You cannot pick up the gems if you only float on the surface." Sri Ramakrishna

In *Living the Yoga Life* Swami Nirmalananda shares the gems he has found from a lifetime of "diving deep." This collection of reflections and short essays addresses the key concepts of yoga philosophy that are so easy to take for granted. Never content with the accepted cliches about yoga sadhana, the yoga life, the place of a guru, the nature of Brahman and our unity with It, Swami Nirmalananda's insights on these and other facets of the yoga life will inspire, provoke, enlighten, and even entertain.

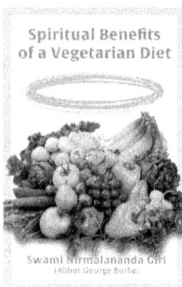

Spiritual Benefits of a Vegetarian Diet

The health benefits of a vegetarian diet are well known, as are the ethical aspects. But the spiritual advantages should be studied by anyone involved in meditation, yoga, or any type of spiritual practice.

Diet is a crucial aspect of emotional, intellectual, and spiritual development as well. For diet and consciousness are interrelated, and purity of diet is an effective aid to purity and clarity of consciousness.

The major thing to keep in mind when considering the subject of vegetarianism is its relevancy in relation to our explorations of consciousness. We need only ask: Does it facilitate my spiritual growth—the development and expansion of my consciousness? The answer is Yes.

BOOKS ON THE SACRED SCRIPTURES OF INDIA

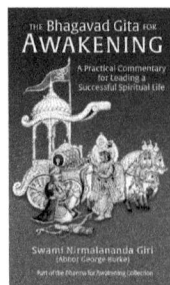

The Bhagavad Gita for Awakening
A Practical Commentary for Leading a Successful Spiritual Life

Drawing from the teachings of Sri Ramakrishna, Jesus, Paramhansa Yogananda, Ramana Maharshi, Swami Vivekananda, Swami Sivananda of Rishikesh, Papa Ramdas, and other spiritual masters and teachers, as well as his own experiences, Swami Nirmalananda illustrates the teachings of the Gita with stories which make the teachings of Krishna in the Gita vibrant and living.

From *Publisher's Weekly*: "[The author] enthusiastically explores the story as a means for knowing oneself, the cosmos, and one's calling within it. His plainspoken insights often distill complex lessons with simplicity and sagacity. Those with a deep interest in the Gita will find much wisdom here."

114

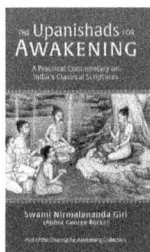

The Upanishads for Awakening
A Practical Commentary on India's Classical Scriptures

The sacred scriptures of India are vast. Yet they are only different ways of seeing the same thing, the One Thing which makes them both valid and ultimately harmonious. That unifying subject is Brahman: God the Absolute, beyond and besides whom there is no "other" whatsoever. The thirteen major Upanishads are the fountainhead of all expositions of Brahman.

Swamiji illumines the Upanishads' value for spiritual seekers from the unique perspective of a lifetime of study and practice of both Eastern and Western spirituality.

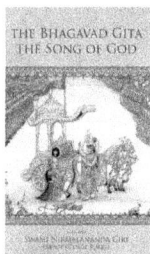

The Bhagavad Gita–The Song of God

Often called the "Bible" of Hinduism, the Bhagavad Gita is found in households throughout India and has been translated into every major language of the world. Literally billions of copies have been handwritten or printed.

The clarity of this translation by Swami Nirmalananda makes for easy reading, while the rich content makes this the ideal "study" Gita. As the original Sanskrit language is so rich, often there are several accurate translations for the same word, which are noted in the text, giving the spiritual student the needed understanding of the fullness of the Gita.

All Is One
A Commentary On Sri Vaiyai R. Subramanian's Ellam Ondre

Swami Nirmalananda's insightful commentary brings even further light to Ellam Ondre's refreshing perspective on what Unity signifies, and the path to its realization.

Written in the colorful and well-informed style typical of his other commentaries, it is a timely and important contribution to Advaitic literature that explains Unity as the fruit of yoga sadhana, rather than mere wishful thinking or some vague intellectual gymnastic, as is so commonly taught by the modern "Advaita gurus."

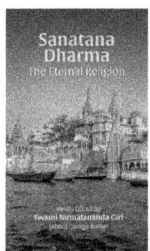

Sanatana Dharma
The Eternal Religion

Sanatana Dharma, commonly called Hinduism, is not just beautiful temples, colorful festivals, gurus and unusual beliefs. It is, simply put, "The Way Things Are" on a cosmic scale. It is the facts of existence and transcendence.

Swami Nirmalananda has edited for the modern reader a book originally printed nearly one hundred years ago in Varanasi, India, for use as a textbook by students of Benares Hindu University. Its original title was *Sanatana Dharma, An Advanced Text Book of Hindu Religion and Ethics*.

A Brief Sanskrit Glossary
A Spiritual Student's Guide to Essential Sanskrit Terms

This Sanskrit glossary contains full translations and explanations of hundreds of the most commonly used spiritual Sanskrit terms, and will help students of the Bhagavad Gita, the Upanishads, the Yoga Sutras of Patanjali, and other Indian scriptures and philosophical works to expand their vocabularies to include the Sanskrit terms contained in these, and gain a fuller understanding in their studies.

BOOKS ON ORIGINAL CHRISTIANITY

The Christ of India
The Story of Original Christianity

"Original Christianity" is the teaching of both Jesus and his Apostle Saint Thomas in India. Although it was new to the Mediterranean world, it was really the classical, traditional teachings of the rishis of India that even today comprise the Eternal Dharma, that goes far beyond religion into realization.

In *The Christ of India* Swami Nirmalananda presents what those ancient teachings are, as well as the growing evidence that Jesus spent much of his "Lost Years" in India and Tibet. This is also the story of how the original teachings of Jesus and Saint Thomas thrived in India for centuries before the coming of the European colonialists.

May a Christian Believe in Reincarnation?
Discover the real and surprising history of reincarnation and Christianity.

A growing number of people are open to the subject of past lives, and the belief in rebirth–reincarnation, metempsychosis, or transmigration–is commonplace. It often thought that belief in reincarnation and Christianity are incompatible. But is this really true? May a Christian believe in reincarnation? The answer may surprise you.

"Those needing evidence that a belief in reincarnation is in accordance with teachings of the Christ need look no further: Plainly laid out and explained in an intelligent manner from one who has spent his life on a Christ-like path of renunciation and prayer/meditation."—Christopher T. Cook

The Unknown Lives of Jesus and Mary
Compiled from Ancient Records and Mystical Revelations

"There are also many other things which Jesus did, the which, if they should be written every one, I suppose that even the world itself could not contain the books that should be written." (Gospel of Saint John, final verse)

You can discover much of those "many other things" in this unique compilation of ancient records and mystical revelations, which includes historical records of the lives of Jesus Christ and his Mother Mary that have been accepted and used by the Church since apostolic times. This treasury of little-known stories of Jesus' life will broaden the reader's understanding of what Christianity really was in its original form.

Robe of Light
An Esoteric Christian Cosmology

In *Robe of Light* Swami Nirmalananda explores the whys and wherefores of the mystery of creation. From the emanation of the worlds from the very Being of God, to the evolution of the souls to their ultimate destiny as perfected Sons of God, the ideal progression of creation is described. Since the rebellion of Lucifer and the fall of Adam and Eve from Paradise flawed the normal plan of evolution, a restoration was necessary. How this came about is the prime subject of this insightful study.

Moreover, what this means to aspirants for spiritual perfection is expounded, with a compelling knowledge of the scriptures and of the mystical traditions of East and West.

116

The Gospel of Thomas for Awakening
A Commentary on Jesus' Sayings as Recorded by the Apostle Thomas

When the Apostles dispersed to the various area of the world, Thomas travelled to India, where evidence shows Jesus spent his Lost Years, and which had been the source of the wisdom which he had brought to the "West."

The Christ that Saint Thomas quotes in this ancient text is quite different than the Christ presented by popular Christianity. Through his unique experience and study with both Christianity and Indian religion, Swami Nirmalananda clarifies the sometimes enigmatic sayings of Jesus in an informative and inspiring way.

The Odes of Solomon for Awakening
A Commentary on the Mystical Wisdom of the Earliest Christian Hymns and Poems

The Odes of Solomon is the earliest Christian hymn-book, and therefore one of the most important early Christian documents. Since they are mystical and esoteric, they teach and express the classical and universal mystical truths of Christianity, revealing a Christian perspective quite different than that of "Churchianity," and present the path of Christhood that all Christians are called to.

"Fresh and soothing, these 41 poems and hymns are beyond delightful! I deeply appreciate Abbot George Burke's useful and illuminating insight and find myself spiritually re-animated." –John Lawhn

The Aquarian Gospel for Awakening (2 Volumes)
A Practical Commentary on Levi Dowling's Classic Life of Jesus Christ

Written in 1908 by the American mystic Levi Dowling, The Aquarian Gospel of Jesus the Christ answers many questions about Jesus' life that the Bible doesn't address. Dowling presents a universal message found at the heart of all valid religions, a broad vision of love and wisdom that will ring true with Christians who are attracted to Christ but put off by the narrow views of the tradition that has been given his name.

Swami Nirmalananda's commentary is a treasure-house of knowledge and insight that even further expands Dowling's vision of the true Christ and his message.

Wandering With The Cherubim
A Commentary on the Mystical Verse of Angelus Silesius–The Cherubinic Wanderer"

Johannes Scheffler, who wrote under the name Angelus Silesius, was a mystic and a poet. In his most famous book, "The Cherubinic Wanderer," he expressed his mystical vision.

Swami Nirmalananda reveals the timelessness of his mystical teachings and The Cherubinic Wanderer's practical value for spiritual seekers. He does this in an easily intelligible fashion for those wishing to put those priceless teachings into practice.

"Set yourself on the journey of this mystical poetry made accessible through this very beautifully commentated text. It is text that submerges one in the philosophical context of the Advaita notion of Non Duality. Swami Nirmalananda's commentary is indispensable in understanding higher philosophical ideas, for Swami's language, while readily approachable, is rich in deep essence of the teachings."–Savitri

BOOKS ON BUDDHISM & TAOISM AND MORE

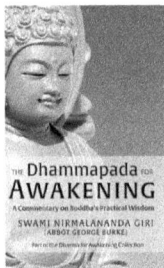

The Dhammapada for Awakening
A Commentary on Buddha's Practical Wisdom

Swami Nirmalananda's commentary on this classic Buddhist scripture explores the Buddha's answers to the urgent questions, such as "How can I find find lasting peace, happiness and fulfillment that seems so elusive?" and "What can I do to avoid many of the miseries big and small that afflict all of us?" Drawing on his personal experience, the author sheds new light on the Buddha's eternal wisdom.

"Swami Nirmalananda's commentary is well crafted and stacked with anecdotes, humor, literary references and beautiful quotes from the Buddha. I have come to consider it a guide to daily living." –Rev. Gerry Nangle

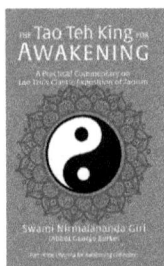

The Tao Teh King for Awakening
A Practical Commentary on Lao Tzu's Classic Exposition of Taoism

"The Tao does all things, yet our interior disposition determines our success or failure in coming to knowledge of the unknowable Tao."

Lao Tzu's classic writing, the Tao Teh King, has fascinated scholars and seekers for centuries. Swami Nirmalananda offers a commentary that makes the treasures of Lao Tzu's teachings accessible and applicable for the sincere seeker.

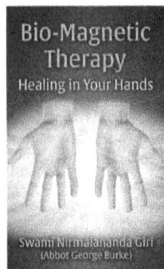

Bio-Magnetic Therapy
Healing in Your Hands

In *Bio-Magnetic Therapy* Swami Nirmalananda teaches the techniques to strengthen your vitality and improve the body's natural healing ability in yourself and in others with specific methods that anyone can use.

Bio-Magnetic Therapy is a simple and natural way to increase the flow of life-force into the body for general good health and to stimulate the supply and flow of life-force to a troubled area that has become vitality-starved through some obstruction. It does not cure; it simply aids the body to cure itself by supplying it with curative force.

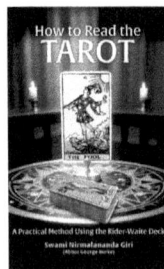

How to Read the Tarot
A Practical Method Using the Rider-Waite Deck

Discover Swami Nirmalananda's unique method of reading the Tarot specifically for use with the Rider-Waite deck, with detailed instructions on how to use the cards to develop your intuition for understanding the meanings of the cards. Illustrated with color plates of each of the cards of the Rider-Waite deck with full explanations of their symbolism.

More Titles
The Four Gospels for Awakening
Light on the Path for Awakening
Light from Eternal Lamps
Vivekachudamani: The Crest Jewel of Discrimination for Awakening

www.ingramcontent.com/pod-product-compliance
Lightning Source LLC
Chambersburg PA
CBHW060314050426
42448CB00009B/1821